Department for Education
Welsh Office
Scottish Office Education Department
Department of Education for Northern Ireland
Universities Funding Council

Education Statistics for the United Kingdom 1992 Edition

Department for Education
Welsh Office
Scottish Office Education Department
Department of Education for Northern Ireland
Universities Funding Council

London: HMSO

ISBN 0 11 270810 2

CONTENTS

INTRODUCTION

This new edition of "Education Statistics for the United Kingdom" updates, mainly to 1990/91, its description of education in the United Kingdom. Its value is as the primary source of education statistics for the UK as a whole, allowing comparisons to be made over time (sometimes as far back as 20 years) and in many of the tables between the 4 home countries. A summary of the main trends evident from the statistics is given in "Summary of Main Tables" immediately following this introduction.

Articles

As in past editions of the volume, special articles are featured on selected topics of general and specific interest. This year there are 3 articles; 2 covering international comparison work (an update of the 'International Comparison' article featured in the 3 previous volumes and a description of an OECD project in which the UK is participating) and another on 'Research into Independent Further and Higher Education' which is being carried out on behalf of the Department.

Changes to main tables

Changes this year have been made in the 'further and higher education' section of the tables where new tables have been introduced and others dropped to better reflect the changing face of the further and higher education sectors. Some table renumbering has been necessary as a result.

Contributions

The efforts of the statistics teams in DFE, Welsh Office, Scottish Office Education Department and Department of Education Northern Ireland, who have contributed data for this volume, are greatly appreciated. In DFE the team responsible for bringing all the data together and producing the volume were Michael Davidson, Tony McLay, Dave Walton, Dave McVean and Andrew Lumley.

Analytical Services Branch
Statistics Division A4
Room 304
Mowden Hall
Staindrop Road
Darlington
DL3 9BG

SUMMARY OF MAIN UNITED KINGDOM STATISTICS

1.   This introduction summarises the main features in the detailed statistical tables. The figures cover the academic year 1990/91 (unless otherwise stated).

Summary

2.   The key findings, mainly for 1990/91, with all figures relating to the UK as a whole are:–

      a.   Over 9 million pupils were taught in schools by half a million teachers; the average pupil/teacher ratio for all schools was 17.0 compared to 22.0 in 1970/71 and 18.2 in 1980/81 (paragraph 5, Table A).

      b.   The number of pupils under 5 receiving education in schools (799 thousand) represented almost 53 per cent of the 3 and 4 year old population (paragraph 6, Table B).

      c.   Amongst home students some 5.8 million were engaged in post–compulsory education; 0.5 million in schools, 4.2 million in further education and over 1 million in higher education. Seventy one per cent studied part–time (paragraph 7, Table C).

      d.   Some 60 per cent of 16-18 year olds participated in education, compared with 52 per cent in 1980/81. Participation at ages 19-20 and 21-24, at 32 per cent and 21 per cent of the age groups respectively, was four percentage points and three percentage points respectively, higher than in 1980/81 (paragraphs 8-10, Table D and bar graph).

      e.   There were nearly 1.2 million students in higher education (home and overseas students combined), of which 45 per cent were women. The inclusion of nursing and paramedic students increases the female enrolments to 48 per cent (paragraph 11, Table E).

      f.   28 per cent of young people aged 17 on 31 August 1990 passed at least one post–GCSE academic qualification (A–level or SCE H–grade (paragraphs 12 and 13, Table F)).

      g.   316 thousand students achieved a higher education qualification in 1989/90; in addition there were some 31 thousand successful completions of nursing and paramedical courses at Department of Health establishments (paragraph 16, Table G).

      h.   There were 637 thousand full–time teaching staff, in schools and publicly funded institutions of whom 54 per cent had graduate status (paragraph 17, Table H).

      i.   Net expenditure by public authorities on education was £27 billion, representing 4.8 per cent of the Gross Domestic Product (paragraph 18, Table J).

      j.   775 thousand students received awards covering maintenance and/or fees for further and higher education courses (paragraph 19, Table K).

k.   Of the countries compared in 1989, the UK pre– and post–compulsory education participation rates, at 64 and 70 per cent respectively were towards the middle of the range. UK expenditure in 1988 as a percentage of GNP was 4.6 per cent, compared with Denmark 7.8 per cent (highest) and Germany 4.2 per cent (lowest) (paragraph 20, Table L).

Background

3.   Statistics for the education systems in England, Wales, Scotland and Northern Ireland are collected and processed separately in accordance with the particular needs of the responsible Departments, ie the Department For Education, the Welsh Office Education Department, the Scottish Office Education Department and the Department of Education Northern Ireland. Each Department makes available a selection of statistics concerning the education services for which it is responsible. Statistics on universities are collected by the Universities' Statistical Record on behalf of the Universities Funding Council.

4.   Basic statistics for the whole of the United Kingdom are assembled to illustrate the size and nature of the educational task throughout the four countries and to facilitate international comparisons. They are published annually for the Department by Her Majesty's Stationery Office.

Schools and pupils – Table A

5.   In the United Kingdom in 1990/91 there were just under 35 thousand schools, of which over 25 thousand were primary or nursery and nearly 5 thousand were secondary schools in the public sector. Over 9 million pupils were taught by just over half a million teachers. The average pupil/teacher ratio for all schools was 17.0 compared to 22.0 in 1970/71. The ratio in public sector primary and secondary schools increased slightly from 1989/90, whilst the public sector nursery schools ratio fell slightly. Both pupil and teacher numbers have been increasing from 1985/86 in public sector primary and nursery schools for the first time since the early 1970s.

Table A: Number of schools, pupils[1], teachers[1] and pupil/teacher ratios within schools

United Kingdom

	Pupil/teacher ratios					1990/91		
	1970/71	1975/76	1980/81	1989/90	1990/91	Pupils (000s)	Teachers (000s)	Schools
Public sector schools								
Nursery	26.6	22.1	21.5	21.8	21.5	60.4	2.8	1,364
Primary	27.1	23.8	22.3	21.7	21.8	4,812.3	220.6	24,135
Secondary[2]	17.8	16.8	16.4	14.8	15.0	3,473.3	232.3	4,790
All	23.2	20.2	19.0	18.1	18.3	8,346.0	455.7	30,289
Non–maintained schools[3]	14.0	14.1	13.2	10.9	10.7	603.8	56.3	2,508
All special schools[4]	10.5	8.7	7.5	5.8	5.7	112.5	19.6	1,824
All schools	22.0	19.4	18.2	16.9	17.0	9,062.3	531.6	34,621

1   Pupils and teachers include full–time equivalents of part–time.
2   With effect from 1989/90 includes voluntary grammar schools (Northern Ireland), previously shown under non–maintained.
3   Includes independent, direct grant and up to 1988/89, voluntary grammar (Northern Ireland).
4   Both public sector and non–maintained. There were 6,400 non–maintained pupils in 1990/91.

Pupils aged under 5 – Table B

6. The number of pupils under 5 receiving education (in all types of school) was 799 thousand in 1990/91, 30 thousand more than in 1989/90 and representing nearly 53 per cent of 3 and 4 year olds (compared with 21 per cent 20 years ago). Much of the increase in participation has been in part–time pupils, although the number of full–time pupils has also increased. Part–time pupils now make up 49 per cent of under 5's in education (21 per cent in 1970/71) and that figure rises to 86 per cent among 2 and 3 year olds.

Table B: Pupils aged under 5[1] attending all types of school

United Kingdom (Thousands)

	All pupils aged under 5[1]							of which aged
	1965/66	1970/71	1975/76	1980/81	1985/86[2]	1989/90	1990/91	2 or 3
Mode of attendance								
Full–time	258	303	392	326	349	394	406	47
Part–time	11	81	184	247	322	375	394	292
All pupils	269	384	576	573	671	769	799	339
Participation rate[3]	14.0	20.5	34.5	44.3	46.7	51.3	52.8	

1   *The age definition used excludes pupils aged 4 at 31 August who became 5 years of age by 1 January.*
2   *Includes 1984/85 data for Scotland.*
3   *As a percentage of all children aged 3 or 4. The numbers of 2 year olds involved are about 5 per cent of the total.*

Post–compulsory education – Tables C and D

7. In 1990/91, some 5.8 million students were engaged in post–compulsory education (excluding those in private colleges) of whom 1.4 million were aged 16–18, 1.3 million aged 19–24 and 2.5 million aged 25 or over. There were also 0.6 million whose age was unknown. Nine per cent of the total number of students were in schools, 72 per cent in further education (including 38 per cent at adult education centres) and 19 per cent in higher education[1]. Seventy one per cent of students aged 16 and over studied part time, while at least 43 per cent were known to be 25 years of age or over. Forty one percent of students aged 16 and over were male but the proportion was larger in higher education (54 per cent) than in further education (36 per cent).

1   *Higher education courses are those reaching standards above GCE A–level, SCE H–grade and BTEC National Diploma or Certificate (or their equivalents).*

4

8.   Thirty–seven per cent of 16–18 year olds in education were in schools, 54 per cent were in further education and 9 per cent were in higher education. Among 19–20 year old students roughly half were in further education and roughly half in higher education. Among older age groups the majority of students were in part–time further education.

Table C: Home students[1] aged 16 and over[2] 1990/91

United Kingdom

	All students (thousands)					Males as a percentage of all students				
	16–18	19–20	21–24	25+	All ages[3]	16–18	19–20	21–24	25+	All ages
All students	1,401	555	752	2,490	5813[4]	51	51	43	33	41[5]
In schools	519	4	–	–	523	49	55	–	–	49
In further education										
Full–time and sandwich	354	38	24	56	472	46	51	50	38	45
Part–time day	280	102	176	783	1,343	69	57	34	25	38
Evening[6]	125	111	300	1,252	2,397[4]	37	38	36	32	33[5]
All FE	759	250	500	2,091	4,213[4]	53	48	36	29	36[5]
In higher education										
Full–time and sandwich	112	265	182	107	667	51	52	55	47	52
Part–time[7]	11	36	71	291	410	69	72	61	53	56
All HE	123	302	253	398	1,077	52	54	57	51	54

1	Excludes students enrolled on nursing and paramedical courses at Department of Health establishments, 81,700 (provisional) in 1990/91; see table D note 1. Excludes students attending private sector colleges.
2	Age at 31 August.
3	Includes sex and ages unknown for Scotland; ages unknown for Wales.
4	Includes students on some courses of adult education for whom age is not known; 605,700 in 1990/91.
5	Based on the total excluding some in adult education (note 4).
6	Includes estimated age for students aged 16 years or more in adult education centres; 1,580,600 in 1990/91.
7	Includes the Open University.

9.   Over 60 per cent of 16 to 18 year olds participated in post–compulsory education in 1990/91 (excluding those in private colleges). Thirty–two per cent of 19 and 20 year olds were continuing with their education. Women aged 16 to 18 were more likely than men of the same age to participate in full–time education. For part–time study, men were more likely to attend on day release, while women were more likely to enter evening classes.

10.   The graph overleaf shows how participation rates among 16–18 year olds have grown since 1980/81. It shows a steady increase in the proportion of this age group participating in education. The increase is largely due to the increase in participation among women. It also shows that the increase has coincided with a shift towards full–time participation especially in the most recent years.

Table D: Percentages of the young adult home population participating in education[1] by sex, age and mode of course, 1990/91

United Kingdom (Percentages)

Age Group (at 31 August)	Mode	1980/81[2] Males	Females	1985/86[3] Males	Females	1988/89 Males	Females	1989/90 Males	Females	1990/91 Males	Females
16–18	Full–time	26.7	31.2	30.5	34.9	34.3	38.5	36.5	41.1	39.7	45.4
	Part–time[4]	26.8	16.7	21.9	18.8	22.8	18.4	22.2	16.8	20.6	15.1
	All	53.5	47.9	52.4	53.7	57.1	56.9	58.7	58.0	60.3	60.5
19–20	Full–time	13.8	11.0	14.6	13.1	15.2	14.1	16.2	15.4	17.7	17.3
	Part–time[4]	17.8	12.1	14.5	13.4	14.2	14.1	14.5	14.4	14.1	14.3
	All	31.6	23.1	29.1	26.5	29.4	28.3	30.6	29.8	31.8	31.5
21–24	Full–time	5.2	3.4	5.0	3.9	5.3	4.4	5.5	4.7	6.0	5.2
	Part–time[4]	11.3	15.9	11.1	16.7	11.0	17.8	11.4	18.1	11.3	18.6
	All	16.5	19.3	16.1	20.6	16.3	22.2	16.9	22.8	17.3	23.8

1   *Includes YT in public sector colleges and adult education centres. Excludes students enrolled on nursing and paramedical courses at Department of Health establishments, 81,700 (provisional) in 1990/91, estimated as 9,000 aged 18, 31,000 aged 19 and 20 and 27,800 aged 21-24; excludes also private sector further education, in–company training and youth clubs and centres.*

2   *Estimated.*

3   *Schools data for Scotland relate to 1984/85.*

4   *Includes the Open University.*

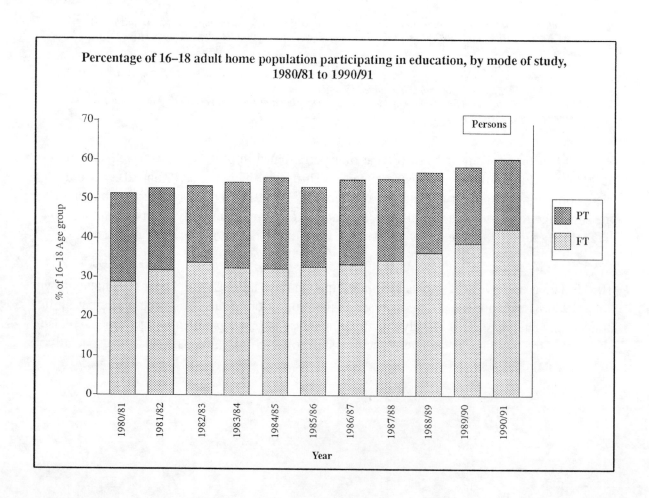

Percentage of 16–18 adult home population participating in education, by mode of study, 1980/81 to 1990/91

Higher education – Table E

11.   The total number of students enrolled in higher education in 1990/91 was nearly 1.2 million. This represents a 42 per cent increase since 1980/81 and an 89 per cent increase over 1970/71 (these figures exclude students on nursing and paramedical courses at Department of Health establishments, 81,700 in 1990/91). The change among women has been much higher than among men, with an increase of 76 per cent since 1980/81 compared to 22 per cent for men. This means that women now make up 45 per cent of higher education enrolments, 8 percentage points higher than in 1980/81 and 12 percentage points higher than in 1970/71. The increase in total enrolments has also been higher in polytechnics and colleges (55 per cent since 1980/81) than in universities (28 per cent). There has also been a sizeable increase in part–time university students, most of whom study with the Open University which started in 1970/71.

Table E: Higher education students enrolled[1] by type of establishment, mode of attendance and sex

United Kingdom

	Thousands						1990/91			Percentage change 1980/81 to 1990/91		
	1956/66	1970/71	1975/76	1980/81	1985/86	1989/90	Persons	Males	Females	Persons	Males	Females
Universities												
Full–time	173	235	269	307	310	351	370	208	162	+21	+ 9	+ 40
Part–time[2]	13	43	82	101	120	143	154	82	72	+52	+37	+ 76
Total	186	278	351	408	430	494	524	290	234	+28	+16	+ 50
Polytechnics and colleges												
Full–time	133	222	247	228	290	338	378[3]	190	187	+66	+50	+ 85
Part–time	110	121	137	192	217	262	274[3]	161	112	+43	+10	+143
Total	243	343	383	420	507	600	652[3]	351	299	+55	+29	+103
All HE establishments[2]												
Total	429	621	734	827	937	1,094	1,176[3]	641	533	+42	+22	+76

1   Includes students from abroad. Excludes students enrolled on nursing and paramedical courses at Department of
      Health establishments, 81,700 (provisional) in 1990/91. Excludes students attending private sector colleges.
2   Includes Open University.
3   Includes sex unknown figures for Scotland.

Qualifications obtained – Tables F and G

12.   A greater proportion of young people now achieve success in public examinations than in the 1970s. The number of school leavers gaining at least 1 GCE A level, 1 SCE H-grade or 2 AS levels is increasing. As a proportion of the population aged 17 at the previous August it rose from 16.6 per cent in 1970/71 to 23.2 per cent in 1990/91. Amongst school leavers in 1990/91 a larger percentage of girls than boys gained at least one of these qualifications – a reverse of the position in 1970/71. The increase for girls has been over nine percentage points since 1970/71. Another 4.9 per cent of the age group obtained A–levels in tertiary colleges and other maintained further education establishments, continuing the increasing trend of A–level passes in further education colleges. In addition a large number of young people gained vocational qualifications, some complementing academic qualifications at further education colleges (see also paragraph 14).

13.　　In addition to those young people who leave school with A–levels, 11.7 per cent of the age group obtained 5 or more higher grade GCSE/O–level (grades A, B or C), CSE grade 1 or equivalent Scottish qualification (SCE O–grade) compared with 7.1 per cent in 1970/71. As a proportion of the population aged 15 at the previous August, 24.8 per cent left school with 1–4 higher grades, compared with 16.8 per cent in 1970/71. In addition a further 24.1 per cent of this age group obtained 1 or more other grade (D–G at GCSE, D or E at O–level, 2–5 at CSE or equivalent in Scotland) compared with 9.8 per cent in 1970/71. Some 7.5 per cent of the age group left school in 1990/91 with no public examination achievements whatsoever, compared with 44.0 per cent in 1970/71. The raising of the school leaving age (on 1 September 1972), the growth in use of the CSE and the introduction of the GCSE (in 1988) have contributed to the substantial increase in the proportion obtaining academic qualifications.

Table F: GCSE/GCE/CSE/SCE attainments of young people as a percentage of the relevant population[1]

| | | | | | | | Males | | Females | |
							United Kingdom (Percentages)			
	1970/71	1975/76	1980/81	1985/86	1989/90	1990/91	1970/71	1990/91	1970/71	1990/91
1 or more GCE A–levels or SCE H–grades[2]										
All students[3]	..	19	20	22	26	28	..	26	..	30
School leavers only	16.6	16.9	17.0	17.8	21.8	23.2	17.8	21.7	15.3	24.7
No A–levels or SCE H–grades (School leavers)[4]										
5 or more higher grades[5]	7.1	8.2	8.9	10.5	11.3	11.7	6.2	10.0	8.0	13.6
1–4 higher grades[5]	16.8	23.9	24.8	26.7	26.2	24.8	16.2	23.8	17.4	25.8
1 or more other grades[6]	9.8	27.8	30.6	32.7	25.4	24.1	10.7	27.0	8.9	21.1
No graded results	**44.0**	**18.7**	**13.5**	**11.7**	**8.3**	**7.5**	**43.9**	**8.7**	**44.1**	**6.2**

1　Based on population aged 17 years at 31 August preceding the academic year for 5 or more higher GCSE/GCE O–level/CSE grades and above, and aged 15 years for other qualification levels.
2　Includes students with 2 AS levels.
3　School pupils and young home students at tertiary and other further education establishments, estimated and rounded to the nearest percentage point.
4　Includes students with 1 AS level.
5　Grades A–C at GCSE/GCE O–level and grade 1 at CSE. Includes Scottish O/S–grades 1–3/A–C.
6　Grades D–G at GCSE, grades D, E at GCE O–level (except 1970/71, when no such award was made) and grades 2–5 at CSE. Includes Scottish O/S–grades 4–5/D–E.

14.　　Only limited information is available on vocational qualifications gained in further education and this area is complicated by multi–part examinations. In 1989/90 some 109 thousand students gained BTEC First and National Certificates, Diplomas and Continuing Education Certificates. Other vocational qualifications gained in further education include those through the City and Guilds of London Institute (340 thousand awards and certificates in 1990/91), SCOTVEC National Certificates (746 thousand full module passes in 1990/91) and the Royal Society of Arts.

15.   Follow up studies such as the Labour Force Survey (LFS) indicate the stock of qualified manpower by age in the population. This avoids the double counting inherent in the Annual output of qualifications. Analyses from the 1991 LFS are included in tables 37 to 39 of this volume.

16.   In 1989/90, 316 thousand students obtained a higher education qualification (table 7). This was 94 thousand more than in 1980/81 and was mainly due to the increase in the number of women gaining such qualifications; almost double the 1980/81 level. In addition, there were some 31 thousand successful completions of nursing and paramedical courses at Department of Health establishments in 1989/90. The proportion of higher education qualifications received which were in science or engineering related subjects was much higher among men (46 per cent) than women (26 per cent). The reverse was true of arts subjects with figures of 29 per cent for women and 15 per cent for men. Amongst all higher education qualifications roughly half were at first degree level or equivalent.

Table G: Higher education qualifications obtained by broad subject group, level and sex[1]

United Kingdom

	Below degree level[2,3]			First degrees[4]			Postgraduate[5]			All		
	Males	Females	Persons	Males	Females	Persons	Males	Females	Persons	Males	Females	Persons
All HE graduates[6] (thousands)												
1980/81	45	17	62	76	48	124	24	13	37	144	78	222
1981/82	46	18	64	76	51	127	24	13	37	146	82	228
1982/83	47	19	66	76	53	129	24	13	36	146	85	231
1983/84	51	22	72	77	56	133	24	13	37	152	91	243
1984/85	54	25	79	80	60	139	26	15	41	160	99	260
1985/86	54	26	80	78	61	139	27	16	42	158	103	262
1986/87	53	32	85	79	64	143	29	17	46	161	113	274
1987/88	50	33	83	80	66	146	30	19	50	160	118	279
1988/89	54	35	89	81	68	149	32	22	54	167	125	292
1989/90	**62**	**45**	**107**	**82**	**70**	**152**	**33**	**24**	**57**	**177**	**140**	**316**
Subject group[6] (Percentages)												
Arts[7]	10	17	13	14	30	21	25	48	35	15	29	21
Science[8]	43	31	38	48	24	37	44	22	35	46	26	37
Social Studies[9]	44	47	45	24	27	25	29	28	28	32	34	33
Other[10]	3	5	4	14	19	17	2	3	3	8	12	10
All subjects[6]	100	100	100	100	100	100	100	100	100	100	100	100

1   *The following refer to calendar years for the second year shown: university diplomas and certificates, CNAA MPhil and PhD degrees; CNAA qualifications prior to 1985/86.*
2   *Includes higher TEC/SCOTEC, BEC/SCOTBEC, BTEC/SCOTVEC, HND/HNC, first university diplomas and certificates, CNAA diplomas and certificates below degree level and estimates of successful completions of public sector professional courses.*
3   *Trends in qualification numbers and enrolments may not be directly comparable because, inter alia, qualifications may not be assigned to the year in which they are achieved.*
4   *Includes university degrees and estimates of: university validated degrees (GB), CNAA degrees (and equivalent) and successful completions of public sector professional courses. Also includes certain CNAA Diplomas in Management Studies.*
5   *Includes universities, CNAA and estimates of successful completions of public sector professional courses. Postgraduate Certificates in Education are included.*
6   *Excludes successful completions of nursing and paramedical courses at Department of Health establishments, 31,000 in 1989/90. Excludes private sector.*
7   *Education; language, literature and area studies; arts other than languages; music, drama, art and design.*
8   *Medicine, dentistry and health; engineering and technology; agriculture, forestry and veterinary science; science; architecture and other professional subjects.*
9   *Administrative, business and social studies.*
10   *Combined and General; Open University.*

Teaching staff – Table H

17.　　In 1990/91 there were 637 thousand full–time teaching staff in schools and publicly funded colleges and universities, 56 thousand fewer than 10 years previously. This fall has mainly been caused by a decrease of 47 thousand in the number of teachers in secondary schools over this period (compared with 12 thousand in primary schools). The percentage of teaching staff with graduate status has increased by 12 percentage points over the same period with the increase being highest in primary schools (19 percentage points). The proportion of graduates among school teachers was lower for women (45 per cent) than men (64 per cent). The proportion of teaching staff who are men was 44 per cent in 1990/91, 4 percentage points lower than in 1980/81. The proportion of men has decreased in all sectors of education. This volume indicates that 11 per cent of teachers were below 30 years of age in 1990/91 compared with 25 per cent in 1979/80.

Table H: Teaching staff by type of establishment, sex and graduate status

United Kingdom

	Public sector schools			All Schools	FHE	Univ	Total[2]
	Primary[1]	Secondary	Total				
Full–time teaching staff　(Thousands)							
1970/71	203	199	402	448	69	29	546
1975/76	240	259	499	555	86	32	677
1980/81	222	281	503	565	89	34	693
1981/82	214	279	493	553	90	34	681
1982/83	207	278	485	545	92	32	672
1983/84	203	276	479	540	93	31	668
1984/85	200	271	471	533	93	31	660
1985/86[3]	201	266	467	529	93	31	657
1986/87[3]	203	262	465	528	93	31	656
1987/88[4]	206	253	459	522	94	31	651
1988/89	209	244	454	518	94	31	643
1989/90	210	239	449	513	90	31	641
1990/91	210	234	444	508	91	32	637
Teaching staff with graduate status　(Percentages)							
1970/71	7	39	23	25	38	..	30[5]
1975/76	10	45	28	29	42	99	34
1980/81	17	54	37	39	43	99	42
1981/82	18	56	39	41	43	99	44
1982/83	20	58	42	43	44	99	46
1983/84	22	60	43	45	44	99	47
1984/85	23	61	45	46	45	99	49
1985/86[3]	25	62	46	47	46	99	50
1986/87[3]	27	63	47	48	47	99	50
1987/88[4]	29	63	48	49	47	99	51
1988/89	29	57	44	46	47	99	52
1989/90	34	65	51	52	48	99	53
1990/91	36	66	52	53	48	99	54
of which Males	45	70	64	64	48	99	65
Females	34	62	45	45	49	99	47
Teaching staff: who are males　(Percentages)							
1970/71	23	57	40	41	81	..	48[5]
1975/76	22	56	40	40	79	91	48
1980/81	22	55	40	41	78	89	48
1981/82	21	55	40	41	78	89	48
1982/83	22	55	41	41	77	89	48
1983/84	21	54	40	41	76	89	48
1984/85	21	54	40	41	75	89	48
1985/86[3]	20	54	40	40	74	88	47
1986/87[3]	20	53	39	39	73	88	46
1987/88[4]	20	53	38	39	73	88	46
1988/89	19	53	38	38	73	87	46
1989/90	18	52	36	37	70	86	44
1990/91	18	52	36	37	69	85	44

1　　　Includes nursery schools.
2　　　Includes unclassified teachers, not elsewhere specified. Excludes private colleges.
3　　　Includes 1984/85 schools data for Scotland.
4　　　Includes 1986/87 data for Northern Ireland.
5　　　Includes estimated data for universities.

Expenditure on education and related services – Table J

18.   In the financial year 1990–91, net expenditure by public authorities on education, including school meals and milk, increased to £26.7 billion. This represented 4.8 per cent of the Gross Domestic Product, which was unchanged from the 1989–90 rate, but was considerably less than in 1975–76, when the number of pupils to be provided for was much higher. The expenditure includes Department of Employment funding through local education authorities.

Table J: Total net UK education and related expenditure

United Kingdom

Financial Year	1965–66	1970–71	1975–76	1980–81	1985–86	1989–90	1990–91[1]
Net expenditure[2]							
Cash (£ million)	1,644	2,740	7,009	12,941	17,288	24,614	26,678
As a percentage of GDP[3]	4.6	5.2	6.4	5.5	4.8	4.8	4.8

1	Provisional.
2	Excludes additional adjustment to allow for capital consumption made for National Accounts purposes amounting to £1,144m in 1990–91.
3	GDP at market prices. Includes adjustments to remove the distortion caused by the abolition of domestic rates which have led to revisions to the historical series.

Student awards – Table K

19.   Provisional figures show that 775 thousand students received awards covering maintenance and/or fees for further and higher education courses in 1990/91, 9.7 per cent higher than the previous year and almost two and a half times the number in 1965/66. Nearly 81 per cent were studying for their first higher education qualification. United Kingdom residents on full–time courses leading to their first higher education qualification are generally eligible for an award which is subject to a parental means test.

Table K: Number of students receiving awards[1]

United Kingdom (thousands)

	1965/66	1970/71	1975/76	1980/81	1985/86	1989/90	1990/91[2]
Type of award[3]							
Postgraduate	..	17	20	21	23	26	26[4]
Full value awards[5] mainly for higher education	..	418	444	447	509	554	625
Paid at 50 per cent or less of the mandatory rate	28	33	45	77	132	126	124[4]
All awards	**320**	**468**	**509**	**546**	**664**	**707**	**775**

1	Sources for awards are Education Departments, Research Councils, LEAs, Universities, Polytechnics, Colleges and other.
2	Provisional.
3	Excludes educational maintenance allowances to school pupils.
4	Includes estimated data for England, Wales and Scotland within a given total.
5	Both mandatory and discretionary awards including discretionary awards at less than (down to 51 per cent) the mandatory rate. Also includes PGCE awards.

International Comparisons – Table L

20.   The period of compulsory education in the UK is among the longest of any country. For some countries with shorter periods of compulsory education this is, however, counterbalanced with relatively high participation rates in pre– and post–compulsory education (eg Belgium and Germany – though compulsory part–time education for 16 and 17 year olds in Germany affects the comparisons). The UK's figures for such participation are in both cases towards the middle of the range when compared with those countries in table L. The percentage of GNP which is spent on education by Governments varies widely, with Germany spending only 4.2 per cent and Denmark 7.8 per cent. The UK rate at 4.6 per cent is in the bottom half of the range.

Table L: International comparisons

Country	Ages of compulsory education	Public expenditure[1] on education as % of GNP CALENDAR YEAR 1988	% of age group in education (FT & PT)	
			3 to 5 1989	16 to 18[2] 1989
Australia	6 to 15[3]	5.0[4]	..	69[5]
Belgium	6 to 14	4.9[6]	96[7]	87[7]
Canada	6 to 16/17	7.1	37	77[8]
Denmark	7 to 16	7.8	..	79[9]
France	6 to 16	5.3	100	81
Germany	6 to 15	4.2	63	92[10]
Italy	6 to 14	4.8[4]	76[7]	65[11]
Japan	6 to 15	4.3[12]	46	79[13]
Netherlands	5 to 16	6.8	65	86[10]
Spain	6 to 16	4.3	69	58
Sweden	7 to 16	6.7	46	75[14]
UK	5 to 16	4.6[15]	64	70[16]
USA	6–8 to 16–18[17]	5.3	55	77[18]

1	Includes subsidies to the private sector.
2	Includes apprenticeships, YTS and similar schemes.
3	6 to 16 in Tasmania.
4	1987 data.
5	Includes an estimate for those studying subsidised courses at non–government business college.
6	Ministry of Education only.
7	1988 data.
8	Excludes certain part–time students (16% at 16–18).
9	Includes an estimate for part–time.
10	Includes compulsory part–time education for 16 and 17 year olds.
11	1982 data.
12	Estimated. Includes some private funding, but excludes fees.
13	Estimated for Special Training and miscellaneous schools providing vocational training.
14	Includes estimated part–time.
15	UK expenditure (converted to calendar year) is expressed as a percentage of GNP and is not directly comparable with expenditure in Table J which is financial year expressed as a percentage of GDP.
16	Includes estimates for those studying only in the evening and for private sector further and higher education, including training courses with employers.
17	Varies between states.
18	1990 data.

INTERNATIONAL COMPARISONS

1.   The Department For Education supply summary statistics for the United Kingdom on a joint questionnaire to the Organisation for Economic Co–operation and Development (OECD), Statistical Office of the European Communities (SOEC) and United Nations Educational, Scientific and Cultural Organisation (UNESCO). Most educational activity is assigned to 7 categories or ISCED[1] levels. The correspondence between figures in the questionnaire and tables in the UK Volume or other publications is described in a note obtainable from the address in paragraph 4.

2.   Comparative tables have been compiled using data supplied by various countries to the international bodies and by direct correspondence. There are inevitably a number of problems of comparability and interpretation in using these tables and readers are advised to read the footnotes carefully. The main aspects needing attention are:

a.   The underlying educational systems need to be understood and the statistics adjusted to a standardised form, if at all possible. As an aid to understanding the differences between various countries, the Department have published two booklets, 'Selected National Education Systems', each describing the main features of 6 developed countries.

b.   The ages at which different stages of education are undertaken varies. In particular the range of compulsory education differs.

c.   Part–time study should be taken into account, and numbers of enrolments adjusted to full–time equivalents in certain contexts.

d.   The range of public and private provision, and the definition of the public/private sectors, will vary from country to country.

e.   Institutions may cover more than one of the education levels, so that estimates are required to assign the figures between levels.

f.   To obtain comparisons for a common year, it is often necessary to adjust figures for academic or financial years. Financial data require updating using consumer price indices and converting to a common basis using purchasing power parities. The dates at which enrolment counts are taken can also affect the figures.

g.   In higher education enrolment rates are misleading for comparisons of participation because of varying course–lengths and drop–out rates. Comparison of new entrants and qualifiers is more meaningful.

---

1   International Standard Classification of Education.

h.   Comparisons between countries of the different levels within higher education are not always very helpful because different countries can interpret the definitions of sub–degree, first degree and post graduate courses differently. In most cases it is best to combine the figures for all three levels. Further problems arise in using figures for the United States, where, for instance, the figures for sub–degree higher education may cover some courses akin to further education in the UK; and Japan, where some further education colleges (senshu) run courses more akin to higher education.

3.   Four sets of international comparisons are presented in tables AA to DD. Table AA covers pre–school education and day–care; the UK is almost unique in commencing compulsory schooling at age 5. Table BB covers education and training at ages 16–18. Most countries have included apprenticeships and training schemes; for compatibility, the UK figures contain an estimate of private sector education and employer training, although these are not routinely covered in statistical returns. Table CC compares participation and qualifications in higher education. For the reasons given above (para 2 (h)), the figures for the USA and Japan are presented as ranges. The UK figures exclude private sector and correspondence courses in higher education; these would add a few percentage points to the UK rates. Table DD compares public expenditure on education.

4.   Copies of the statistical bulletins referred to at the foot of each table can be obtained from:

Room 338
Mowden Hall
Staindrop Road
Darlington DL3 9BG   Telephone 0325-392683

A note on the ISCED levels and on the derivation of data for international returns can be obtained from Room 304, Mowden Hall, Staindrop Road, Darlington, DL3 9BG, telephone 0325 392753/6. This same contact can supply copies of the descriptive booklets on the different educational systems (SNES I and II) and can deal with general queries.

Participation in Education and Day Care of 3 to 5 year olds

–   Participation is usually highest among children just before compulsory school age. Age 6 is the usual compulsory school starting age. The exceptions are UK and Netherlands at 5, Scandinavia at 7 and 8 in some states of the USA.

–   In Belgium and France virtually all 3 to 5 year olds participated in education. The United Kingdom was in an intermediate position with participation rates of 64 per cent in education in 1989, rising to 66 per cent in 1991.

–   Almost all countries have increased the participation in the education of 3 to 5 year olds since 1982, with the UK having one of the largest percentage changes of the countries compared.

TABLE AA: PARTICIPATION IN EDUCATION OF 3 TO 5 YEAR OLDS, 1989[1]: AGE PARTICIPATION RATES

Percentages

	Age at which compulsory schooling starts	EDUCATION							DAY CARE
Age:		3	4	5	3 to 5		3 to 4		3 to 5
Year		1989			1982	1989	1982	1989	1987[2]
Belgium[1]	6	94	98	97	97	96	96	96	–
Canada	6	–	42	70	34	37	13	21	9[2]
Finland[1]	7	16	20	24	..	20	..	18	33[2]
France	6	97	100	100	97	100	95	99	–
Germany	6	33	72	85	60	63	51	52	
Ireland	6	1	53	96	50	51	27	27	14[2]
Italy[1,3]	6	70	80	79	76	76	76	76	–
Japan	6	17	56	64	45	46	33	37	29[2]
Netherlands	5	..	98	99	66	65	50	49	17[2]
Norway	7	34	47	56	..	46	..	40	43
Spain	6	17	89	100	..	69	..	53	–
Sweden	7	39	44	56	35	46	..	42	20
UK[4]	5	35	58	100	61	64(66[5])	43	46(50[5])	27[6]
USA	6–8[7]	27	51	86	52	55	36	39	..

..   not available
–   nil or negligible

1.   *1988 data for Belgium, Finland and Italy.*
2.   *Day Care data: 1985 for Canada, 1983 for Finland, Ireland and Netherlands, 1986 for Japan.*
3.   *Estimated.*
4.   *Revised.*
5.   *1991 data.*
6.   *DFE estimates (via General Household Survey) including day nurseries, playgroups, mother and toddler clubs, but avoiding double counting with education.*
7.   *Various between states.*

SEE ALSO STATISTICAL BULLETIN 13/89

Education and Training of 16 to 18 year olds

– Participation rates for 16 to 18 year olds as a whole are variable, ranging from 58 per cent in Spain to 92 per cent in Germany; the UK level of 69 per cent was lower than most other countries in 1988, although it rose to 70 per cent in 1989.

– A higher proportion of 16 year olds undertake some kind of education or training; the United Kingdom level of 91 per cent in 1988 was similar to that in other countries and rose to 93 per cent in 1989.

– There are larger differences between countries in full–time participation rates than in overall rates. The UK has the lowest full–time participation rate, but the second highest part–time participation rate.

TABLE BB: PARTICIPATION IN EDUCATION AND TRAINING[1] OF 16 TO 18 YEAR OLDS BY AGE, MODE AND LEVEL, 1989: AGE PARTICIPATION RATES

Percentages

	Minimum leaving age	16 years			16 to 18 years		
		Full–time	Part–time	All	Full–time	Part–time	All[3]
Australia[4]	15[5]	76	12	85	52	17	69
Belgium[2]	14	92	4	96	82	4	87
Canada[6]	16/17	100	–	100	77	–	77
Denmark[7]	16	89	2	90	73	6	79
France	16	82	8	89	73	8	81
Germany[8]	15	71	29	100	49	43	92
Italy[2]	14	54	15	69	47	18	65
Japan[9]	15	93	1	94	76	3	79
Netherlands[8]	16	93	5	98	77	9	86
Spain	16	68	–	68	58	–	58
Sweden[7]	16	84	1	85	73	2	75
United Kingdom[10]	1988 16	50	41	91	35	34	69
	1989 16	53	41	93	36	33	70
USA[2]	16–18[11]	95	–	95	75	2	77

1   *Includes apprenticeships, YTS and similar schemes.*
2   *1988 for Belgium; 1983 for Italy; 1990 for USA.*
3   *Includes higher education for some 18 year olds.*
4   *Includes an estimate for those students studying subsidised courses at non–government business colleges.*
5   *16 in Tasmania.*
6   *Excludes certain part–time students, 16% at 16–18.*
7   *Part–time estimated.*
8   *Includes compulsory part–time education for 16 and 17 year olds in Germany and Netherlands.*
9   *Includes private sector higher education and an estimate for special training and miscellaneous schools providing vocational training.*
10   *Includes estimates for those studying only in the evening and for private sector further and higher education, including training courses with employers.*
11   *Varies between states.*

SEE ALSO STATISTICAL BULLETIN 1/90

Higher Education

– The new entrant participation rate in higher education varied from 30 per 100 of the relevant year group in Italy to over 50 per 100 in Australia, and the upper part of the range in both Japan and the USA. The UK rate (excluding the private sector) was 37 per 100, rising to 41 in 1990.

– The number of UK higher education qualifications gained when standardised and expressed as an index was 32 per 100, above the equivalent figures for Australia and most European countries considered, including Germany and Netherlands, but lower than those for the USA, Canada, France and Japan. Higher figures for Japan and USA in both measures include courses which may be below level 5.

– The final column shows the success (or conversely wastage) rates for those entering higher education. The data shows the UK ratios to be amongst the highest of the 13 countries.

TABLE CC: HIGHER EDUCATION NEW ENTRANT AND QUALIFICATION RATES

	Typical Length of Course (Years)		New Entrant Rate[1]	Qualification Rates[2]		Qualifications Awarded per 100 New Entrants
			1989	1988		1987
	First Degree (Level 6)	Sub–Degree (Level 5)	All HE	Levels 5 & 6	All Levels	Levels 5 & 6
Australia[3]	5	2	57	28	30	62
Belgium	4	2	49[5]	35	38	86[4]
Canada	5	2	59[5,6]	44	49	92
Denmark	6	3	48	22[4]	22	87
France	4	2	44	37[7]	43[7]	..[8]
Germany, Fed Rep	6	3	32	21	23	94[4]
Italy	5	2	30	8	10	33
Japan[9] (a)	4	2	37	35	36	92
(b)[10]	4	2	51	47	49	90
Netherlands	5	4	36[11]	28[4]	28	69[4]
Spain	5	3	38	17	17	92
Sweden	4	3	47[12]	31[4]	32[4]	..
United Kingdom[13]	3	2	37[14](41)[15]	27[16](28)[15]	32[16](34)[15]	90[14,16]
USA[9] (a)	4	2	65	35[18]	45[18]	86[19]
(b)[17]			33	34[18]	33[18]	60[19]

1   OECD define new entrants to higher education as excluding postgraduates and those already qualified in higher education irrespective of age. The denominator is the age–group of the population including 70 per cent of new entrants, divided by the number of years involved.
2   Annual flow of students qualifying, divided by the new entrant denominator aged by typical course length.
3   Excludes Technical and Further Education (TAFE)
4   Level 6 Qualifier data includes level 7.
5   1987 data for Canada, 1988 for Belgium.
6   Provisional.
7   Increased by level 5 diplomas awarded on the completion of the first two years of a level 6 course.
8   Because of some double counting in the qualifier data (see footnote 7), a meaningful comparison with new entrant data is not possible.
9   Includes data for private colleges and correspondence courses.
10   Includes advanced students in special training schools (SENSHU's) some of whose courses may be equivalent to level 5.
11   Full–time only and excludes Open University.
12   Excluding one–year courses which may be below level 5.
13   Excludes private HE.
14   Excludes postgraduates and students from abroad. Includes nursing and paramedical entrants at DH establishments.
15   1990 data. 1989 qualification rates shown in brackets.
16   Includes estimated public sector professional qualifications and nursing and paramedical qualifications gained at DH Establishments.
17   Excludes students on two–year courses (some of which may be below level 5), and, where appropriate, transfers Bachelor's and Master's degrees to level 5 and 6 respectively.
18   1987 data.
19   1986 data.

See also INTERNATIONAL COMPARISONS OF HIGHER EDUCATION: WORKING REPORT

Public Expenditure on Education

–   Various measures of public expenditure on education are shown below. Spain had low ratings on most of the measures, while Canada, Denmark and the Netherlands were amongst the highest. The UK occupied an intermediate position on most of the measures, similar to that of Germany.

–   Higher education expenditure (which includes student support and research) showed particular diversity; public expenditure per qualifier in Netherlands and Denmark was over 4 times higher than in Spain and around twice that in UK and Germany.

TABLE DD: PUBLIC EXPENDITURE ON EDUCATION (FOR CALENDAR YEAR SHOWN)

	Start of financial year	Years of Full–time Compulsory Education	Total public education expenditure[1] as % of GNP	Public Recurrent expenditure[1,2] per capita		HE Recurrent expenditure[1,2] per qualifiers £000s
				Below HE level £	HE £	
			1988	1988		1988
Australia	JUL	9[3]	5.0[4]	220[4]	110[4]	24.8[4]
Belgium	JAN	8	4.9[5]	280	70	12.0
Canada	APR	10	7.1	420	210	27.0
Denmark	JAN	9	7.8	410	130	35.9
France	JAN	10	5.3	310	50	8.5
Germany, Fed	JAN	9(11)[6]	4.2	230	70	18.6
Italy	JAN	8	4.8[4]	260[4]	40[4]	26.1[7]
Japan[9,12]	APR	9	4.3	200[4]	30[4]	28.3[7,14]
Netherlands	JAN	11(12)[6]	6.8	280	160	32.6
Spain	JAN	10	4.3	180	50	7.1[4,8]
Sweden	JUL	9	6.7	380	80	16.3
UK	APR	11	4.6 (4.7)[10]	280	70	15.7[11]
USA[9,12] (a)	OCT	11[13]	5.3	390	140	18.0[7,14]
(b)[15]				410	120	21.2[7,14]

1   *Includes subsidies to the private sector.*
2   *At purchasing power parity for the calendar year shown. Earlier years uprated using consumer price indices.*
3   *10 years in Tasmania.*
4   *1987 data.*
5   *Ministry of Education only.*
6   *Bracketed figures include compulsory part–time education for young leavers.*
7   *1986 data.*
8   *3rd level qualifiers estimated for Spain.*
9   *Estimated. Includes some private funding, but excludes fees.*
10   *1990 data*
11   *Excludes expenditure on students at Department of Health establishments on nursing and paramedical courses. Also excludes in–service teacher training secondments.*
12   *Japan and USA data on public recurrent expenditure has been estimated.*
13   *Varies between states.*
14   *Excludes subsidies to the private sector and private graduates.*
15   *The USA ranges show the effect of transferring 2 year courses from higher to further education (see also Table CC).*

18

OECD's EDUCATION AT A GLANCE

1.   There is a growing demand from governments, researchers and the general public in OECD member countries for international comparisons of educational performance. In an effort to meet this demand, the International Educational Indicators (INES) project was launched by OECD and its Centre for Educational Research and Innovation (CERI). The project has operated with a network of groups, each addressing specific sectors of indicators and with the aim of proposing, formulating and calculating indicators in their own areas, which fit into the indicator system as a whole.

2.   In combination, the indicators are intended to provide skeletal pictures of each country's education system thus providing more fruitful sets of comparisons than simple league tables of, for example, which country spends most on education. In essence, the INES framework of indicators aims to provide a ready made diagnostic tool to aid policy making and policy monitoring. The project is long–term and the development of the full set of indicators within the framework is ongoing, but, an initial selection of the indicators, some more finalised than others, was published by OECD in **Education at a Glance (EAG) on 23 September 1992**.

3.   The indicators published in Education at a Glance are divided into three main areas:

> 1.   **Demographic, Economic and Social Context**: seen as important background factors that condition the flow of financial and human resources available for education. Five indicators are presented;
>
> 2.   **Cost resources and school process**: seen as the mediating variables that, to a greater or lesser extent, provide an indication as to the importance attached by OECD countries to investment in education; 21 indicators are presented;
>
> 3.   **Outcomes of Education**: always reflect the historical conditions of education and the combined effects of the policies, programmes, practices and decisions constituting schooling in each country. 10 indicators are presented.

4.   The indicators, themselves, cover most areas of education, including:

> –   the level of education in the population;
> –   participation of various levels of education;
> –   Expenditure on education
> –   graduates by subject

5.   The scope of this first edition, based on 1988 data, is still limited, but future editions will expand on the range of indicators. Work is already under way to collect the next series of data for Education at a Glance, which is likely to be published some time in late 1993. Concurrent work is also ongoing to prepare new indicators from both the technical groups and the networks. OECD hope that these new indicators will appear in Education at a Glance 3, which is planned for Autumn 1995.

Expenditure per pupil and GDP per capita – Table A

6.   Table A, shows a reproduction of one of the most interesting indicators featured in EAG (Indicator P7), which shows education expenditure per student by source in relation to per capita GDP and by level of education. The indicator places the figures on expenditure per student in relative perspective comparing them against a broad measure of the standard of living of people in each country. One might expect that education expenditure per student of a country would closely correlate with the wealth of its inhabitants (measured here by GDP per Capita). Figures 1 and 3 showing education up to secondary level provides some evidence in support of this, but the tertiary level graphs (figures 2 and 4) do not suggest such a strong relationship at that level (UK data are missing from figures 3 and 4 because of the lack of data available on private expenditure on education).

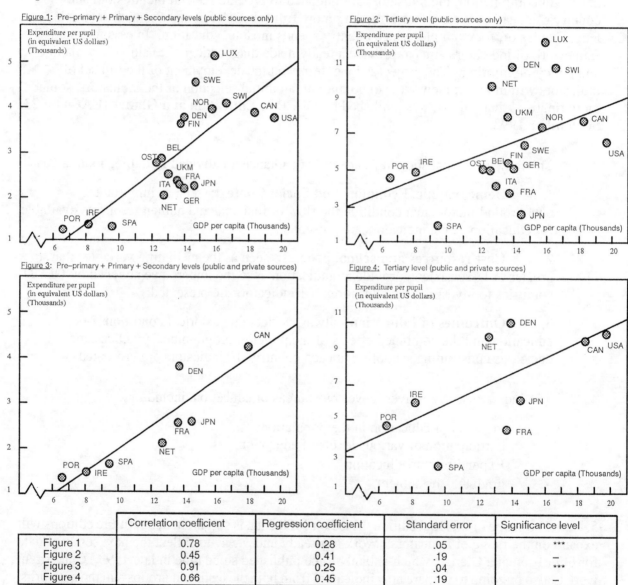

Figure 1: Pre–primary + Primary + Secondary levels (public sources only)

Figure 2: Tertiary level (public sources only)

Figure 3: Pre–primary + Primary + Secondary levels (public and private sources)

Figure 4: Tertiary level (public and private sources)

	Correlation coefficient	Regression coefficient	Standard error	Significance level
Figure 1	0.78	0.28	.05	***
Figure 2	0.45	0.41	.19	–
Figure 3	0.91	0.25	.04	***
Figure 4	0.66	0.45	.19	–

Note: This is a reproduction of the graphs as they appear in EAG and have not been plotted from the actual underlying data. Some minor inaccuracies may therefore be present.

Statistics Division A4
Analytical Services Branch
Department For Education

December 1992

RESEARCH INTO INDEPENDENT FURTHER AND HIGHER EDUCATION

Introduction

1.   In their 1979 report on a study of independent further and higher education Williams and Woodhall[1] concluded private colleges and vocational schools catered for between one fifth and one sixth of all students over the age of 16 in Britain. This illustrated the size and importance of the independent sector at the time and until recently has largely been the basis for estimating overall participation rates in education and thus allowing more comparable international comparisons of participation to be made in that area. The need to update this research was clear and in 1991 the Department For Education with supporting finance from the Welsh Office and the Scottish Office Education Department commissioned the Centre for Higher Education Studies at the Institute of Education, University of London to do so. This note gives an account of the research so far and the preliminary findings that are emerging.

Scope of the Sector

2.   In preparing for the survey the scope of the sector was defined as:

> All independent institutions in Great Britain providing further and higher education on a systematic basis to students above the minimum school leaving age and which do not already make a statistical return to the Department For Education, the Scottish Office Education Department or the Welsh Office.

3.   Foreign universities and colleges based on British soil were included as was training carried out in Government/NHS training establishments and a sample of systematic training provided by the largest 200 or so companies where the training is provided in a separate establishment.

Methods

4.   The research has been in 3 stages:

   i.   *Compilation of a register of providers* – this has involved detailed examination of lists of institutions obtained from various sources eg training directories, professional qualification directories and awarding bodies, eliminating where possible at this stage those institutions out of scope of the research.

   ii.   *Postal Survey* – of the 7,000 or so institutions generated from stage i. a sample of some 4,900 were selected and postal questionnaires despatched to them. Initially some 2,000 questionnaires were returned (meeting the researchers target of a 40 per cent response rate) and telephone follow ups

---

1.   "Independent Further Education", Gareth Williams and Maureen Woodhall, 1979, Policy Studies Institute

21

have been underway to increase the response and to establish the characteristics of the non-respondents.

iii.   *Analysis of the results* – this has begun and is due to be completed in the Spring of 1993 with a formal report to the Departments of the findings of the research.

Preliminary Results

5.   As data cleaning is still underway the following are very much provisional results but are useful in giving a broad indication of the size of the numbers involved in the sector:

Independent further and higher education, 1992 (Provisional)

Country	No of Institutions	Students participating during Survey week (11 May 1992) (000s)	Total Students participating in year ending 30 April 1992 (000s)
England	3,866	504	1,742
Scotland	198	15	59
Wales	174	13	48
Total GB	4,238	533	1,850

6.   Thus, a little over half a million students participated (full–time, part–time or correspondence courses) in independent further and higher education at some four thousand institutions during the survey week in May 1992. Throughout the whole year up to the end of April 1992 the total number of students who had participated was over $1^3/_4$ million.

Statistics Division A4
Analytical Services Branch
Department For Education

December 1992

22

MAIN UNITED KINGDOM TABLES

TABLE 1: Population by age and sex (1) at 1 January

Thousands

	1971	1976	1981(2)	1986(2)	1990(2)	1996(2)	1991(2) UK	England	Wales	Scotland	N I	
MALES												**MALES**
2	471	396	336	368	390	412	401	333	20	34	14	2
3	477	416	328	366	385	410	391	324	20	34	14	3
4	485	443	341	373	385	406	385	319	19	33	14	4
5	492	447	353	377	370	400	385	319	19	33	14	5
6	500	453	369	368	371	395	371	306	19	32	14	6
7	487	463	393	337	369	402	372	307	19	33	14	7
8	480	471	418	329	376	391	369	304	18	33	13	8
9	464	479	449	342	380	386	376	310	19	34	13	9
10	452	486	444	354	370	387	380	314	20	33	14	10
11	432	495	457	370	340	372	371	306	19	33	13	11
12	427	482	464	393	332	373	340	281	17	30	13	12
13	417	476	474	419	344	371	332	273	17	30	12	13
14	402	462	481	449	356	378	345	282	18	32	13	14
15	387	451	495	445	372	383	357	293	19	33	13	15
16	391	439	497	457	396	374	373	307	19	34	13	16
17	393	434	483	463	421	344	397	327	20	36	14	17
18	389	424	473	474	449	336	422	349	21	37	15	18
19	393	412	462	481	444	350	450	373	22	40	15	19
20	..	401	449	496	456	362	445	368	22	41	15	20
21-24	..	1,590	1,675	1,921	1,903	1,645	1,868	1,553	88	170	57	21-24
25-29	1,865	2,129	1,929	2,084	2,343	2,281	2,389	1,996	115	214	65	25-29
30 and over	..	14,380	14,885	15,179	15,583	16,699	15,716	13,185	791	1,368	372	30 and over
Total Population	..	26,629	26,655	26,845	27,133	27,854	27,235	22,726	1,360	2,396	752	Total Population
FEMALES												**FEMALES**
2	448	368	320	350	372	392	382	317	19	32	13	2
3	454	391	311	347	365	390	372	308	19	32	13	3
4	460	421	324	355	366	386	366	302	18	32	13	4
5	468	423	335	359	352	380	366	303	19	32	13	5
6	475	429	349	348	353	375	352	291	18	30	13	6
7	465	440	371	319	350	381	353	291	18	31	13	7
8	456	447	396	311	357	372	351	289	18	32	13	8
9	442	453	426	324	361	365	358	294	18	32	13	9
10	430	463	420	335	350	366	362	298	19	32	13	10
11	410	469	434	350	322	352	351	289	17	31	13	11
12	406	459	440	371	313	353	322	265	16	29	12	12
13	396	451	448	396	325	351	313	257	16	28	12	13
14	382	439	456	426	337	358	326	266	17	31	12	14
15	369	429	468	421	352	362	338	277	17	31	12	15
16	374	415	470	434	373	352	353	290	18	32	12	16
17	379	412	460	441	400	324	374	308	19	34	13	17
18	377	403	456	450	429	316	400	331	20	37	13	18
19	381	390	448	461	425	330	431	357	22	39	13	19
20	..	378	434	474	439	342	427	353	21	40	13	20
21-24	..	1,518	1,627	1,868	1,837	1,572	1,802	1,501	86	164	51	21-24
25-29	1,820	2,073	1,892	2,043	2,295	2,218	2,335	1,953	117	204	60	25-29
30 and over	..	16,409	16,927	17,174	17,518	18,462	17,627	14,719	898	1,582	428	30 and over
Total Population	..	28,080	28,212	28,357	28,591	29,099	28,659	23,862	1,449	2,566	782	Total Population
PERSONS(3)												**PERSONS(3)**
2	919	760	656	718	762	804	782	650	39	66	28	2
3	931	807	639	713	750	799	763	632	38	66	28	3
4	945	864	665	727	751	792	751	621	38	65	27	4
5	960	870	689	736	722	780	752	623	38	64	27	5
6	975	882	718	716	724	770	723	598	36	62	27	6
7	952	903	763	657	719	783	725	598	37	64	27	7
8	936	918	814	640	733	763	720	593	36	64	26	8
9	906	932	875	666	741	752	734	604	37	67	27	9
10	882	949	864	690	720	753	742	612	39	65	27	10
11	842	964	890	720	661	724	721	595	36	64	26	11
12	833	941	904	764	644	727	662	546	33	59	25	12
13	813	927	922	815	670	722	645	530	34	58	24	13
14	784	901	937	874	694	736	671	548	35	63	25	14
15	756	880	962	866	724	745	695	570	36	64	25	15
16	765	854	967	892	769	725	726	597	37	66	26	16
17	772	846	943	905	821	668	771	635	39	71	27	17
18	766	827	929	924	878	653	822	680	41	74	27	18
19	774	802	910	942	870	679	881	730	44	80	28	19
20	..	779	882	970	895	704	872	722	42	80	27	20
21-24	..	3,108	3,302	3,789	3,740	3,217	3,670	3,054	174	333	108	21-24
25-29	3,685	4,202	3,822	4,127	4,638	4,499	4,724	3,949	233	418	125	25-29
30 and over	..	30,789	31,811	32,355	33,100	35,161	33,342	27,904	1,689	2,949	800	30 and over
Total Population	..	54,705	54,864	55,206	55,723	56,953	55,893	46,588	2,809	4,962	1,534	Total Population

(1) Population based on demographic data provided by the Office of Population Censuses and Surveys and the Government Actuary's Department. Estimated for 1971 to 1990; estimated/projected for 1991; projected for 1996.

(2) Age at 31 August the previous year.

(3) Males and Females may not sum to Persons totals due to rounding.

ALL INSTITUTIONS

TABLE 2: Number of schools(1) or departments by type and establishments of higher and further education

			Academic years(2)				
		1965/66	1970/71	1975/76	1980/81	1985/86	1989/90	1990/91
UNITED KINGDOM								
Public sector -	Nursery	604	723	1,040	1,251	1,262	1,337	1,364
	Primary	26,881	26,799	26,981	26,504	24,756	24,268	24,135
	Secondary	6,636	6,010	5,625	5,542	5,161	4,876	4,790
	of which 6th form colleges (E+W)	-	12	68	101	109	115	116
Non-maintained		3,699	3,096	2,760	2,640	2,538	2,492 (3)	2,508 (4)
Special		1,054	1,204	1,913	2,011	1,923	1,853 (5)	1,830
Universities (including Open University)(6)		43	48	48	48	48	48	48
PCFC Sector:	Polytechnics	-	26	31	31	30	30	32
	Other(7)	.	.	.	.	.	56	53
Other HE/ FE: Vocational colleges and Colleges of Education(8)								
	Public sector	..	1,038	889	744	697	594 (5)	587
	Assisted	108	110	95	62	56	26 (5)	26
Adult education centres (England and Wales only)		7,455	6,502	7,260	4,628	2,874 (9)	2,669	2,656
ENGLAND								
Public sector -	Nursery	421	454	564	588	560	564	566
	Primary	20,751	21,083	21,394	21,018	19,549	19,162	19,047
	Secondary	5,412	4,984	4,728	4,654	4,286	3,976	3,897
	of which 6th form colleges	-	12	67	100	108	113	114
Non-maintained		3,495	2,754	2,442	2,342	2,274	2,283 (3)	2,289 (4)
Special		868	983	1,545	1,593	1,493	1,398	1,380
Universities (including Open University)(6)		36	37	37	37	37	37	37
PCFC Sector:	Polytechnics	-	25	29	29	29	29	31
	Other(7)	.	.	.	.	.	56	53
Other HE/ FE establishments								
	Maintained and assisted	841 (10)	687	573	468	436	375	370
	Grant-aided	79 (10)	78	66	35	31	6	6
Adult education centres		7,455 (10)	5,061	5,976	4,067	2,616 (9)	2,399	2,315
WALES								
Public sector -	Nursery	41	44	67	69	59	55	54
	Primary	2,071	1,990	1,959	1,908	1,774	1,729	1,717
	Secondary	386	311	254	239	237	231	230
	of which 6th form colleges	-	-	1	1	1	2	2
Non-maintained		103	74	71	72	69	67	71
Special		34	36	73	73	67	63 (5)	61
Universities		1	1	1	1	1	1	1
Polytechnics		-	1	1	1	1	1	1
Other HE/ FE establishments								
	Maintained and assisted	-	59	54	44	39	36	36
	Grant-aided	-	3	2	1	1	1	1
Adult education centres		-	1,441	1,284	561	258 (9)	270	341
SCOTLAND								
Public sector -	Nursery	124	201	373	515	559	633	659
	Primary	2,646	2,497	2,507	2,522	2,425	2,378	2,372
	Secondary	647	510	439	444	440	429	424
Non-maintained		..	173	160	138	106	123	131
Special		129	159	264	319	339	346 (5)	343
Universities		5	8	8	8	8	8	8
Vocational further and higher education colleges								
	LEA: Day	76	85	70	65	50	46	46
	LEA: Evening	213	146	132	109	115	110	110
	Central institutions	13	13	14	14	16	13	13
	Voluntary bodies	5	4	1	-	-	-	-
Colleges of education		9	10	10	10	7	5	5
NORTHERN IRELAND								
Grant-aided -	Nursery	18	24	36	79	84	85	85
	Primary	1,413	1,229	1,121	1,056	1,008	999	999
	Secondary(11)	191	205	204	205	198	240	239
Non-maintained(12)		101	95	87	88	89	19	17
Special(13)		23	26	30	26	24	46	46
Universities		1	2	2	2	2	2	2
Colleges of education		4	4	3	3	2	2	2
Ulster Polytechnic		-	-	1	1	-	-	-
Further education colleges		- (14)	33	28	26	26	26	24

(1) See paragraphs 2.2 and 10.1 to 10.9 of the explanatory notes on type of school.
(2) Starting in the Autumn of each year.
(3) Includes 3 City Technology Colleges (CTC's).
(4) Includes 7 City Technology Colleges (CTC's).
(5) Revised figures.
(6) Including London Business School and Manchester Business School, which were previously excluded. See paragraphs 12.2(i) and 12.7 of the explanatory notes.
(7) 56 Institutions transferred from the LEA maintained and grant aided sector w.e.f. 1989/90.
(8) See paragraph 12.2(ii) of the explanatory notes.
(9) Excludes youth clubs and centres; these were included in years prior to 1985/86.
(10) England and Wales.
(11) W.e.f. 1989/90 Includes voluntary grammar schools formerly allocated to the independent sector.
(12) Excludes Voluntary grammar schools allocated to the maintained sector w.e.f. 1989/90.
(13) From 1988/89 includes 22 schools which were the responsibility of the Northern Ireland Department of Health and Social Services up to 31 March 1987.
(14) Not available on a basis comparable to later years.

TABLE 3: New student awards, by type (1)

	Academic years						Thousands
	1965/66	1970/71	1975/76	1980/81	1985/86	1989/90	1990/91 (2)
Postgraduate awards							
Made by							
Education Departments and the Research Councils	..	8.2	8.6	10.4	9.5	9.4	10.7 (3)
Local education authorities (4)	..	1.2	1.9	2.2	3.9	4.8 (5)	4.6 (5)
Undergraduate and non-graduate awards at University	..	58.0	64.4	74.5	71.9	81.0	88.3
Teacher training awards	..	50.7	46.7	21.2	18.9	23.0	26.1
Other awards, including polytechnics and colleges first degree and comparable courses (6), other further and higher education courses	..	50.9	66.6	79.6	102.1	124.3	143.5
Awards paid at 50 per cent or less of the mandatory rate	18.8	26.0	33.8	55.5	90.2	86.0 (5)	89.2 (5)
ALL NEW AWARDS	114.5	195.0	222.0	243.4	296.6	328.6	362.4

(1) See section 8 of the explanatory notes.
(2) Provisional.
(3) Includes 1989/90 data for England and Wales.
(4) Postgraduate course awards made under Section 2 of the Education Act 1962 (excluding initial teacher training) in England and Wales.
(5) Includes estimates for Scotland.
(6) "Comparable courses" are courses at establishments of further and higher education which have been designated under the University and Other Awards
    Regulations, 1965, as comparable to first degree courses.

TABLE 4: Current student awards, by type (1)

	Academic years						Thousands
	1965/66	1970/71	1975/76	1980/81	1985/86	1989/90	1990/91 (2)
Postgraduate awards							
Made by							
Education Departments and the Research Councils	..	15.9	17.7	19.0	18.9	19.1	19.3 (3)
Local education authorities (4)	..	1.4	2.1	2.3	4.4	7.1 (5)	6.9 (5)
Undergraduate and non-graduate awards at University	..	179.3	193.0	231.1	225.4	240.6	263.7
Teacher training awards	..	132.5	121.4	44.1	39.4	45.6	51.4
Other awards, including polytechnics and colleges first degree and comparable courses (6), other further and higher education courses	..	105.9	129.6	171.8	244.5	267.9	310.1
Awards paid at 50 per cent or less of the mandatory rate	27.5	32.8	44.8	77.3	131.6	126.2 (5)	123.8 (5)
ALL CURRENT AWARDS	320.1	467.8	508.6	545.7	644.3	706.5	775.3

See footnotes at Table 3 above.

FINANCE

TABLE 5: Summary of net education and related expenditure

	Financial year 1 April to 31 March (1)						£ million
	1965-66	1970-71	1975-76	1980-81	1985-86	1989-90	1990-91(2)
Local education authorities							
Education							
Recurrent(3)	988.3	1,599.7	4,579.5	8,975.9	12,264.6	16,978.9	18,573.3
Capital	152.2	282.9	535.6	568.9	495.5	789.3	821.0
Total	1,140.5	1,882.6	5,115.1	9,544.8	12,760.1	17,768.2	19,394.3
Loan charges(4)	119.6	216.5	455.9	769.3	793.6	873.9	861.7
Related							
Recurrent	210.1	324.0	832.0	1,410.6	1,846.1	2,072.0	2,234.6
Capital	17.7	19.6	28.8	17.2	20.3	30.0	23.7
Total	227.8	343.6	860.9	1,427.8	1,866.4	2,102.0	2,258.3
Loan charges(4)	7.5	14.1	23.3	34.4	35.7	35.9	41.4
Education Departments(5)							
Education							
Recurrent(3),(6)	37.0	66.1	242.9	516.4	673.1	931.8	1,053.8
Capital	20.7	29.5	51.5	56.8	80.9	161.0	215.2
Total	57.5	95.6	294.4	573.2	754.0	1,092.8	1,269.0
Loan charges(4), (7)	-	-	6.7	6.1	5.1	4.9	5.1
Related							
Recurrent	17.5	26.0	47.5	99.2	101.5	116.9	197.4
Capital	3.7	2.7	8.5	6.5	3.1	2.5	2.0
Total	21.2	28.7	56.0	105.7	104.6	119.5	199.4
Grants through PCFC							
Education							
Recurrent	.	.	.	.	.	1,023.5	1,016.0
Capital	.	.	.	.	.	90.1	88.3
Total	.	.	.	.	.	1,113.6	1,104.3
Grants through UFC(8)							
Education							
Recurrent	118.8	226.5	525.9	987.0	1,381.4	1,817.7	1,800.8
Capital	78.3	71.3	103.3	113.3	137.6	193.2	208.6
Total	197.1	297.6	629.2	1,100.3	1,519.0	2,010.9	2,009.4
All public authorities							
Education							
Recurrent	1,144.0	1,892.3	5,348.3	10,479.3	14,319.2	20,751.9	22,443.9
Capital	251.3	383.7	690.4	739.0	714.0	1,233.3	1,333.2
Total	1,395.3	2,275.9	6,038.7	11,218.3	15,033.2	21,985.2	23,777.1
Related(9)							
Recurrent	227.6	350.0	879.6	1,509.8	1,947.6	2,188.9	2,432.0
Capital	21.4	22.3	37.3	23.7	23.4	32.5	25.7
Total	249.0	372.3	916.9	1,533.5	1,971.0	2,221.4	2,457.7
All expenditure							
Recurrent	1,371.7	2,242.3	6,227.9	11,989.2	16,266.8	22,940.8	24,875.9
Capital	272.6	406.0	727.7	762.6	737.4	1,265.8	1,358.9
Total	1,644.3	2,648.2	6,955.6	12,751.8	17,004.2	24,206.6	26,234.8
Loan charges(4)	127.1	230.6	485.9	809.8	834.4	914.7	908.2
SET/VAT(10),(11) incurred on above expenditure	-	92	53	189	284	407	443
All public expenditure on education(12) (including school meals and milk)	1,644	2,740	7,009	12,941	17,288	24,614	26,678
Gross national product (at market prices)(10)	37,041	53,781	112,204	237,347	367,067	527,421	556,201
Gross domestic product (GDP, at market prices)(10),(13)	35,952	52,231	109,224	233,468	357,901	516,384	554,693
Education expenditure as a percentage of GDP	4.6	5.2	6.4	5.5	4.8	4.8	4.8
GDP deflator(10),(13)	11.361	14.573	27.641	54.619	74.384	92.607	100.000
GDP in real terms	316,451	358,409	395,152	427,448	481,153	557,608	554,693
Total education expenditure in real terms	14,471	18,802	25,357	23,693	23,241	26,579	26,678

(1) In Scotland prior to 1975-76 the financial year for most education authorities was 16 May to 15 May. In 1975-76 the local authority financial year ended 31 March and the expenditure was therefore grossed up from 10.5 to 12 months for that year only.

(2) Provisional.

(3) With effect from 1 April 1989 includes expenditure on fees for Polytechnics and Colleges transferred to the Polytechnics and Colleges Funding Council.

(4) Not included in total expenditure. See paragraph 7.6 of the explanatory notes.

(5) Including from 1968-69 grants to the Open University.

(6) From 1 April 1971, the expenditure on salaries of certain categories of teacher in Northern Ireland formerly shown under the heading 'local education authorities' has been shown under 'Education Departments'.

(7) From 1 October 1973 the Department of Education, Northern Ireland, has taken over responsibilities for loan charges.

(8) Including corresponding grants in Northern Ireland.

(9) Excludes salaries of teachers seconded for further training, included from 1987-88 under 'Education'.

(10) Source: Central Statistical Office.

(11) Current and Capital VAT.

(12) Excludes additional adjustment to allow for Capital consumption made for National Accounts purposes amounting to £1,144m in 1990-91.

(13) Includes adjustments to remove the distortion caused by the abolition of domestic rates which have led to revisions to the historical series.

TABLE 6: Summary of net education and related expenditure by type of service(1)

	Financial year 1 April to 31 March (2)					£ million
	1970-71	1975-76	1980-81	1985-86	1989-90	1990-91(3)
EDUCATION EXPENDITURE						
Nursery schools (4)						
Recurrent	6.8	25.2	51.9	74.1	..	..
Capital (revenue and/or loans)	1.2	12.4	6.3	8.1	..	..
Total	7.9	37.6	58.2	82.2	..	..
Loan charges	0.2	1.6	4.0	3.4	..	..
Primary schools (4)						
Recurrent	545.9	1,535.6	2,839.8	3,701.6	5,888.2	6,457.6
Capital (revenue and/or loans)	97.8	175.2	173.5	163.7	314.1	353.1
Total	643.8	1,710.8	3,013.3	3,865.3	6,202.3	6,810.6
Loan charges	60.8	138.1	226.1	229.3	280.4	276.5
Secondary schools (4)						
Recurrent	619.5	1,873.4	3,694.8	5,060.7	6,832.2	7,147.4
Capital (revenue and/or loans)	135.0	268.2	274.6	222.7	396.5	464.7
Total	754.4	2,141.6	3,969.4	5,283.4	7,228.7	7,612.0
Loan charges	101.1	213.3	369.3	360.8	379.9	363.4
Special schools						
Recurrent	49.7	186.7	443.5	666.7	1,008.4	1,120.7
Capital (revenue and/or loans)	10.5	35.0	26.0	17.2	37.9	36.1
Total	60.3	221.6	469.5	683.9	1,046.3	1,156.8
Loan charges	5.8	17.1	33.7	33.1	34.7	33.0
Higher,further and adult education(5)						
Student grants (tuition fees)	8.1	19.7	138.7	167.6	257.0	477.9
Other recurrent (inc Training of Teachers - tuition(6))	317.1	859.6	1,530.9	2,307.7	2,447.8	2,633.9
Capital (revenue and/or loans)	68.7	90.7	131.2	151.1	158.5	141.3
Total	393.9	969.9	1,800.6	2,626.4	2,863.3	3,253.1
Loan charges	42.5	78.1	135.1	164.2	141.4	136.2
Polytechnics and Colleges Funding Council						
PCFC Grants - recurrent	.	.	.	.	1,023.5	1,016.0
Capital(revenue)	.	.	.	.	90.1	88.3
Total	.	.	.	.	1,113.6	1,104.3
Universities(6)						
Student grants (tuition fees)	18.3	30.1	217.1	159.8	213.7	385.8
Grants to universities - recurrent(7)	228.1	547.9	1,047.4	1,445.4	1,890.6	1,879.6
Capital (revenue)	71.3	105.6	117.0	140.4	195.6	210.7
Total	317.7	683.6	1,381.5	1,745.6	2,299.9	2,476.0
Other education expenditure						
Recurrent	94.5	270.3	515.5	735.6	1,190.5	1,325.0
Capital(revenue and/or loans)	1.9	3.3	10.4	10.8	40.7	39.0
Loan charges	2.2	7.5	7.2	7.9	42.2	57.6
TOTAL EDUCATION EXPENDITURE						
Total Recurrent	1,888.1	5,348.3	10,479.3	14,319.2	20,751.9	22,443.9
Capital (revenue and/or loans)	386.3	690.4	738.9	714.0	1,233.3	1,333.2
Total	2,274.3	6,038.7	11,218.2	15,033.2	21,985.2	23,777.1
Loan Charges	216.5	462.6	775.4	798.7	878.6	866.8
RELATED EXPENDITURE						
Meals and milk						
Recurrent	115.5	383.1	479.2	532.1	484.6	506.1
Capital (revenue and/or loans)	12.7	16.4	3.0	1.4	1.7	1.7
Total	128.2	399.5	482.2	533.5	486.3	507.8
Loan charges	6.8	13.2	19.2	15.4	14.2	16.3
Youth service and physical training						
Recurrent	23.0	72.3	147.9	238.8	327.8	347.7
Capital (revenue and/or loans)	7.5	18.7	19.2	20.3	26.1	18.7
Total	30.4	91.0	167.1	259.1	353.9	366.4
Loan charges	3.3	7.9	14.9	20.0	21.2	18.8
Transport of pupils (8)	33.9	99.6	215.0	279.4	337.2	396.5
Maintenance grants and allowances to students/pupils (9),(10)	124.7	284.4	630.4	837.9	933.3	1,027.5
TOTAL RELATED EXPENDITURE(11),(12)						
Recurrent	350.0	879.6	1,509.8	1,947.6	2,189.0	2,432.0
Capital (revenue and/or loans)	22.5	37.3	23.7	23.4	32.5	25.7
Total	372.5	916.9	1,533.5	1,971.0	2,221.5	2,457.7
Loan charges	14.1	23.3	34.4	35.7	35.9	41.4

(1) For all expenditure, refer to Table 7.

(2) In Scotland prior to 1975-76 the financial year for most education authorities was 16 May to 15 May. In 1975-76 the local authority financial year ended 31 March and the expenditure was therefore grossed up from 10.5 to 12 months for that year only.

(3) Provisional.

(4) Refer to Table 7 footnote (2).

(5) With effect from 1 April 1989 includes expenditure on fees only for Polytechnics and Colleges transferred to Polytechnics and Colleges Funding Council.

(6) Expenditure on University Departments of Education is included under 'Universities' for England and Wales, but under 'Training of teachers' for Northern Ireland.

(7) Central government expenditure comprises grants administered by the UFC together with a grant by Education Departments to the Open University.

(8) Includes £3.2 million capital expenditure (see Table 7) in 1990-91.

(9) From 1986-87, excludes the secondment of teachers on further training. These have been reallocated to the various sectors. From 1987-88 includes cost of board and lodging for teacher training in England and Wales, ie now all UK.

(10) Includes £74M for student loans in GB.

(11) For 1970-71 and 1975-76 figures include loans.

(12) For all years, includes school welfare and miscellaneous expenditure not shown above.

FINANCE

TABLE 7:   Net education and related expenditure by type of service

Financial year 1 April 1990 - 31 March 1991 (1)   £ million

	Local education authorities	Central govern- ment	Total		Local education authorities	Central govern- ment	Total
(i). EDUCATION EXPENDITURE							
Nursery and primary schools (2)				**Polytechnics and Colleges**			
Recurrent				**Funding Council**			
Salaries and wages				Grants to PCFC			
Teaching staff	4,198.8	169.1	4,367.9	Recurrent - Other	-	1,016.0	1,016.0
Other staff	887.7	-	887.7	Capital from revenue	-	88.3	88.3
Other	1,201.7	0.3	1,202.0	Total	-	1,104.3	1,104.3
Total	6,288.2	169.4	6,457.6				
Capital from revenue	45.6	49.3	94.9	**Universities (3)**			
Capital from loans	258.2	-	258.2	Grants to students - tuition fees	339.1	46.7	385.8
Total	6,591.9	218.7	6,810.6	Grants to universities (4)			
Loan charges	276.5	-	276.5	Recurrent - other	0.2	1,879.4	1,879.6
				Capital from revenue	-	210.7	210.7
Secondary schools				Total	339.3	2,136.8	2,476.0
Recurrent							
Salaries and wages				**Other education expenditure**			
Teaching staff	4,668.2	193.9	4,862.1	Recurrent			
Other staff	684.7	-	684.7	Administration			
Other	1,481.0	119.5	1,600.5	Salaries and wages			
Total	6,834.0	313.4	7,147.4	Teaching staff	58.3	-	58.3
Capital from revenue	56.8	131.0	187.9	Other staff	501.7	10.7	512.4
Capital from loans	273.7	3.1	276.8	Other	481.2	93.3	574.5
Total	7,164.4	447.6	7,612.0	Total	1,041.1	104.0	1,145.3
Loan charges	363.4	-	363.4	Other	100.1	79.7	179.9
				Total recurrent	1,141.3	183.9	1,325.0
Special schools				Capital from revenue	6.3	7.9	14.2
Recurrent				Capital from loans	24.3	0.5	24.8
Salaries and wages				Total	1,171.9	192.3	1,364.2
Teaching staff	525.9	11.7	537.6	Loan charges	52.5	5.1	57.6
Other staff	253.5	0.0	253.5				
Other	324.5	5.0	329.5	**TOTAL EDUCATION EXPENDITURE**			
Total	1,104.0	16.7	1,120.7	Recurrent			
Capital from revenue	4.3	1.7	6.0	Salaries and wages			
Capital from loans	30.1	-	30.1	Teaching staff	11,195.5	425.5	11,620.9
Total	1,138.3	18.4	1,156.8	Other staff	2,899.0	10.9	2,910.0
Loan charges	33.0	-	33.0	Other	4,478.8	3,434.2	7,913.0
				Total	18,573.3	3,870.6	22,443.9
Higher, further and adult education				Capital from revenue	146.8	508.4	655.3
Grants to students - tuition fees(9)	432.3	45.6	477.9	Capital from loans	674.2	3.7	677.9
Other recurrent				Total	19,394.3	4,382.8	23,777.1
Salaries and wages				Loan charges	861.7	5.1	866.8
Teaching staff	1,744.3	50.8	1,795.1				
Other staff	571.3	0.2	571.5				
Other (inc T.T. tuition) (3)	118.6	148.6	267.2				
Total	2,866.6	245.2	3,111.8				
Capital from revenue	33.9	19.5	53.4				
Capital from loans	87.8	0.1	87.9				
Total	2,988.3	264.8	3,253.1				
Loan charges	136.2	-	136.2				

(1) Provisional.

(2) Pre-school and secondary education in primary schools is included under 'Nursery and primary schools'.

(3) Education expenditure on University Departments of Education is included under 'Universities' for England and Wales, but under 'Training of teachers' for Northern Ireland.

(4) Central government expenditure comprises grants administered by the Universities Funding Council together with a grant by Education Departments to to the Open University.

(5) From 1 October 1973 the Department of Education, Northern Ireland, has taken over responsibility for loan charges from the local authorities.

(6) Expenditure mainly on other education's support services in England and Wales. Health programmes fund school health completely in Northern Ireland and Scotland from 1973 and 1974 respectively.

(7) Includes costs of board and lodging.

(8) The totals shown under recurrent expenditure are net expenditure figures. Salaries and wages of 'Teaching and Other' staff are however gross amounts expended by local authorities. Any income has been deducted from 'Other'.

(9) With effect from 1 April 1989 includes expenditure on fees for Polytechnics and Colleges transferred to Polytechnics and Colleges Funding Council.

TABLE 7 (continued): Net education and related expenditure by type of service

Financial year 1 April 1990 - 31 March 1991 (1)

£ million

	Local education authorities	Central govern-ment	Total		Local education authorities	Central govern-ment	Total

(ii). RELATED EXPENDITURE

School welfare (6)				**TOTAL RELATED EXPENDITURE**			
Recurrent				Recurrent			
Salaries and wages				Salaries and wages			
Teaching staff	52.5	-	52.5	Teaching staff	112.2	-	112.2
Other staff	70.8	-	70.8	Other staff	397.5	2.0	399.5
Other	32.0	-	32.0	Other	1,724.9	195.4	1,920.3
Total	155.3	-	155.3	Total	2,234.6	197.4	2,432.0
Capital from revenue	0.1	-	0.1	Capital from revenue	7.5	2.0	9.4
Capital from loans	1.6	-	1.6	Capital from loans	16.3	-	16.3
Total	157.0	-	157.0	Total	2,258.3	199.4	2,457.7
Loan charges	6.4	-	6.4	Loan charges	41.4	-	41.4
Meals and milk				**(iii). ALL EXPENDITURE**			
Recurrent				Recurrent			
Salaries and wages				Salaries and wages			
Teaching staff	-	-	-	Teaching staff (8)	11,307.7	425.5	11,733.2
Other staff	173.8	0.6	174.4	Other staff (8)	3,296.4	12.9	3,309.3
Other	330.9	0.7	331.6	Other	6,203.7	3,629.6	9,833.3
Total	504.8	1.3	506.1	Total	20,807.9	4,068.0	24,875.9
Capital from revenue	1.6	0.1	1.7	Capital from revenue	154.3	510.4	664.7
Capital from loans	-	-	-	Capital from loans	690.4	3.7	694.2
Total	506.4	1.4	507.8	Total	21,652.6	4,582.2	26,234.8
Loan charges	16.3	-	16.3	Loan charges	903.1	5.1	908.2
Youth service and physical training							
Recurrent				**EXPENDITURE IN 1989-90: REVISIONS TO TOTALS**			
Salaries and wages							
Teaching staff	59.7	-	59.7	**Nursery and primary schools**			
Other staff	153.0	0.8	153.8	Recurrent - Other	+194.6	-	+194.6
Other	127.0	7.2	134.2	**Secondary schools**			
Total	339.7	8.0	347.7	Recurrent - Other	+349.0	-	+349.0
Capital from revenue	2.7	1.5	4.0	**Higher, further and adult education**			
Capital from loans	14.7	-	14.7	Capital from loans	-5.6	-	-5.6
Total	356.9	9.5	366.4	**Other education expenditure**			
Loan charges	18.8	-	18.8	Recurrent - Other (non-admin)	-4.4	-	-4.4
				Special Schools			
Transport of pupils				Recurrent - Other	+19.1	-	+19.1
Recurrent	393.3	-	393.3	**Youth Service and Physical Training**			
Capital from revenue	3.2	-	3.2	Capital from Loans	-0.8	-	-0.8
Total	396.5	-	396.5	**Transport of Pupils**			
				Recurrent	+30.6	-	+30.6
Maintenance grants and allowances to				**Maintenance Grants and allowances**			
pupils and students				Other Further Education	-0.4	-	-0.4
Student Loans	-	74.2	74.2				
Universities	219.7	46.8	266.5	**Net changes**			
Training of Teachers: grants and				Recurrent	+588.5	-	+588.5
allowances to students(7)	68.5	12.6	81.1	Capital	-6.4	-	-6.4
Other higher education	382.6	48.2	430.8	Loan charges	+29.7	-	+29.7
Other further education	131.1	4.0	135.1				
Schools (inc special education)	39.8	-	39.8	**Totals**			
Total maintenance grants	841.6	185.8	1,027.5	Recurrent	19,050.9	3,889.9	22,940.8
				Capital	819.0	446.8	1,265.8
				Total	19,869.9	4,336.7	24,206.6
Miscellaneous expenditure				Loan charges	909.8	4.9	914.7
Recurrent							
Salaries and wages							
Teaching staff	-	-	-				
Other staff	-	0.5	0.5				
Other	-	1.7	1.7				
Total	-	2.2	2.2				
Capital from revenue	-	0.4	0.4				
Capital from loans	-	-	-				
Total	-	2.6	2.6				
Loan charges	-	-	-				

For notes see previous page.

TEACHING STAFF

TABLE 8: New entrants, total enrolments and successful students for initial teacher training by sex and type of course(1)

Thousands

	1965	1970	1975	1980	1985	1989	1990
UNITED KINGDOM							
New entrants(2)							
University Departments of Education	3.8	5.3	5.5	6.2	5.0	7.4	8.2
Courses for graduates	3.7	5.1	5.0	5.7	4.3	6.1	7.1
Courses for non-graduates	0.1	0.2	0.5	0.6	0.6	1.3	1.1
Other major establishments	36.3	48.1	42.2	15.7	14.3	18.2	20.1
Courses for graduates	1.7	4.4	7.8	7.0	4.8	6.1	7.0
Courses for non-graduates	34.6	43.7	34.4	8.7	9.5	12.1	13.1
Enrolments(3)							
University Departments of Education	3.8	5.4	6.0	7.7	6.6	9.6	11.1
Courses for graduates	3.7	5.1	5.0	5.7	4.4	6.1	7.1
Courses for non-graduates	0.1	0.3	0.9	2.0	2.2	3.5	4.0
Other major establishments	83.4	125.3	113.2	35.1	33.0	39.3	43.7
Courses for graduates	1.7	4.4	7.9	7.0	4.8	6.2	7.1
Courses for non-graduates	81.7	120.8	105.3	28.0	28.1	33.1	36.6
Successfully completing(4),(5)							
University Departments of Education	3.6	4.6	4.8	5.5	4.9	5.5	5.6
Courses for graduates	3.6	4.6	4.5	4.8	4.3	4.9	5.1
Courses for non-graduates	0.1	0.1	0.3	0.6	0.6	0.6	0.5
Other major establishments	21.9	37.1	42.2	19.4	10.6	11.9	12.2
Courses for graduates	1.6	3.3	6.5	6.2	4.6	5.5	5.7
Courses for non-graduates	20.3	33.8	35.8	13.1	6.0	6.4	6.5
ENGLAND AND WALES(5)							
All new entrants	34.8	46.6	40.8	18.9	17.3	22.9	25.0
Males	11.2	14.7	13.3	7.1	5.1	6.5	7.0
Females	23.6	31.9	27.5	11.8	12.2	16.4	18.0
All enrolments	76.5	115.6	104.3	35.8	34.9	43.2	48.1
Males	23.2	33.8	29.9	10.9	8.5	10.4	11.2
Females	53.3	81.8	74.4	24.9	26.4	32.8	36.9
All successfully completing(6)	21.7	35.9	40.7	21.3	13.8	15.6	15.9
Males	7.8	11.0	13.4	5.9	3.9	4.6	4.4
Females	13.9	24.9	27.3	15.4	9.9	11.0	11.4
SCOTLAND(6)							
All new entrants	4.6	5.7	5.8	2.4	1.4	2.0	2.6
Males	1.0	1.5	1.9	0.8	0.3	0.4	0.6
Females	3.6	4.2	3.9	1.7	1.1	1.6	2.0
All enrolments	8.6	12.2	11.3	4.9	3.0	3.8	4.8
Males	1.0	2.3	2.9	1.3	0.6	0.6	0.8
Females	7.6	9.9	8.4	3.6	2.4	3.2	4.0
All successfully completing	3.1	4.9	5.3	2.7	1.2	1.1	1.3
Males	0.8	1.2	1.5	0.8	0.3	0.2	0.3
Females	2.3	3.7	3.8	1.9	0.9	0.9	1.0
NORTHERN IRELAND							
All new entrants	0.8	1.2	1.4	0.6	0.6	0.7	0.7
Males	0.3	0.4	0.5	0.2	0.1	0.2	0.2
Females	0.5	0.8	0.9	0.4	0.5	0.6	0.6
All enrolments	2.2	2.8	3.5	2.1	1.6	1.8	1.9
Males	0.7	0.9	1.1	0.6	0.3	0.3	0.3
Females	1.5	1.9	2.4	1.5	1.3	1.5	1.5
All successfully completing	0.7	0.9	1.0	0.9	0.6	0.7	0.7
Males	0.2	0.3	0.3	0.3	0.2	0.1	0.1
Females	0.5	0.6	0.7	0.6	0.4	0.5	0.5

(1) See paragraphs 9.1 - 9.6 of the explanatory notes.
(2) Calendar year.
(3) October/November of year shown.
(4) Academic year ending in year shown.
(5) Including students in England and Wales who failed their BEd degree course but have received qualified teacher status on the basis of a non-degree qualification obtained in an earlier year.
(6) Numbers for males and females are estimated from 1980.

TABLE 9: Teachers and lecturers by type of establishment, sex and graduate status: percentage trained

(i) Full-time

	1965/66(1)		1970/71		1975/76		1980/81		1985/86(2)		1989/90(3),(4)		1990/91(3)		
	All 000s	% Graduate	All 000s	% Graduate	All 000s	% graduate	All 000s	% Graduate	All 000s	% Graduate	All 000s	% Graduate	All 000s	% Graduate	% Graduates trained(5)
UNITED KINGDOM															
MALES															
Public sector schools															
Primary(6)	37	7.4	47	11.9	52	15.9	48	23.6	41	33.5	38	42.7	38	45.0	97.7
Secondary(7)	87	39.7	114	42.6	146	48.9	154	57.5	143	65.0	125	68.9	121	69.8	91.1
Non-maintained(7),(8)	3	75.7	17	68.7	19	70.6	20	77.9	21	82.4	20	84.9	21	85.6	..
Special	3	9.1	4	11.2	6	15.4	6	24.5	6	34.9	6	41.4	6	42.9	95.3
All schools	130	30.8	182	36.4	223	42.2	229	51.2	211	59.8	190	64.5	186	65.6	78.4
FHE establishments(9)	36	38.8	56	39.0	68	42.3	70	43.2	69	46.0	63	47.4	62	47.9	57.0
Universities(10)	..	..	..	..	29	99.4	30	98.9	28	99.0	27	99.2	27	99.3	..
All establishments(11)	168	32.7	238	37.0	323	47.2	332	53.8	310	60.1	283	63.7	277	64.8	62.8
FEMALES															
Public sector schools															
Primary(6)	104	3.1	156	5.3	188	8.5	174	14.6	160	22.9	171	32.0	173	34.2	97.8
Secondary(7)	61	30.0	85	34.0	113	39.1	127	49.3	123	58.3	115	61.7	113	62.4	92.2
Non-maintained(7),(8)	3	51.4	19	34.5	20	38.8	23	50.4	22	56.1	23	57.8	24	58.2	..
Special	4	7.6	6	10.7	11	11.5	13	20.4	13	29.3	13	33.3	13	34.0	95.7
All schools	172	13.5	266	16.7	332	20.8	336	30.3	318	39.1	322	44.5	322	45.8	85.3
FHE establishments(9)	8	31.3	13	35.5	17	38.5	19	41.5	24	46.4	27	48.7	28	48.8	65.2
Universities(10)	..	..	..	..	3	98.8	4	98.5	4	98.9	4	99.1	5	99.2	..
All establishments(11)	181	14.3	279	17.6	354	22.4	361	31.5	347	40.2	358	45.3	360	46.5	81.3
PERSONS															
Public sector schools															
Primary(6)	141	4.2	203	6.9	240	10.1	222	16.5	201	25.0	210	34.0	210	36.1	97.8
Secondary(7)	148	35.7	199	38.9	259	44.6	281	53.8	266	61.9	240	65.5	234	66.2	91.6
Non-maintained(7),(8)	6	63.6	36	50.7	39	54.3	43	63.3	43	69.1	44	70.4	45	70.8	..
Special	7	8.2	10	10.9	17	12.9	19	21.7	19	31.1	19	35.8	19	36.8	95.5
All schools	302	20.9	448	24.7	555	29.4	565	38.8	529	47.4	512	51.9	508	53.1	82.2
FHE establishments(9)	44	37.4	69	38.3	86	41.5	89	42.8	93	46.1	90	47.8	91	48.2	59.6
Universities(10)	22	..	29	..	32	99.3	34	98.9	31	99.0	31	99.2	32	99.2	..
All establishments(11)	371	23.2	546	26.5	677	34.2	693	42.2	657	49.6	641	53.4	637	54.5	71.7
ALL SCHOOLS															
ENGLAND AND WALES(3)															
Males	130	30.8	162	33.7	197	39.8	202	49.6	186	58.9	168	63.8	164	65.0	..
Females	172	13.5	226	15.3	284	20.0	288	30.1	274	39.5	278	45.1	278	46.5	..
Persons	302	20.9	388	23.0	481	28.1	490	38.8	460	47.3	446	52.2	442	53.3	..
SCOTLAND(3),(8)															
Males	..	..	15	63.9	19	65.5	20	67.4	..	..	15	70.3	15	71.1	..
Females	..	..	30	27.5	36	27.7	37	30.7	..	..	33	36.8	32	37.8	..
Persons	..	..	45	45.7	55	46.6	57	49.1	..	..	48	47.5	47	48.4	..
NORTHERN IRELAND(3),(7)															
Males	..	..	6	35.8	7	48.9	7	53.7	7	59.9	7	67.9	7	68.9	..
Females	..	..	9	17.7	11	21.5	12	33.4	11	42.5	12	50.1	12	52.3	..
Persons	..	..	15	26.8	18	35.2	19	42.4	18	49.2	19	56.5	19	58.2	..

(ii) Part-time(12)

	1965/66(1)		1970/71		1975/76		1980/81		1985/86(2)		1989/90(3),(4)		1990/91(3)		
GREAT BRITAIN(13)															
Persons	36	..	43	..	44	..	..	..	..	..	..	..	..	..	..
Persons - full-time equivalent	17	..	21	..	21	..	41	..	43	..	53	..	55 (14)	..	..
Schools	17	..	21	..	21	..	17	..	18	..	29	..	30	..	..
FHE establishments	..	..	..	..	..	..	22 (15)	..	23	..	23	..	25	..	..

(1) England and Wales only except universities; excluding independent schools.
(2) In 1985/86 includes 1984/85 schools data for Scotland.
(3) Includes some estimated data for each of the countries.
(4) Includes revised data for England and Wales.
(5) GB only. In Scotland all teachers are required to be trained.
(6) Including nursery schools.
(7) W.e.f. 1989/90 Voluntary Grammar schools in N. Ireland are recorded in the maintained sector.
(8) Excluding independent schools in Scotland.

(9) Excluding Ulster Polytechnic. See Paragraph 9.10 of the explanatory notes for graduate shortfall.
(10) Excluding Open University. There were 697 professors and lecturers and 6,167 part-time tutorial and counselling staff at January 1991.
(11) Including teachers classified as miscellaneous. There were over 2,400 males and over 4,100 females in 1990-91. For England and Wales they are not elsewhere specified but for N. Ireland 25 males, 129 females are also included under 'Special'.
(12) See paragraphs 9.8 - 9.11 of the explanatory notes.
(13) Excluding Universities
(14) Consisting of approximately 22,800 men and 32,100 women.
(15) England and Wales only.

TEACHING STAFF

TABLE 10[11]: Full-time graduate teachers and lecturers by type of establishment, sex and degree subject(1), 1989/90(2)

Thousands

	Medicine & dentistry	Allied medicine	Biological sciences	Agriculture	Physical sciences	Mathematical sciences	Engineering & technology	Architecture	Social sciences
ENGLAND AND WALES									
MALES									
Schools(3)									
Public Sector									
Primary	-	-	0.4	-	0.5	0.3	0.1	-	1.7
Secondary	-	0.1	4.1	0.3	10.1	5.1	2.6	-	8.6
Special	-	-	0.1	-	0.1	-	-	-	0.3
Total schools	-	0.1	4.6	0.3	10.7	5.4	2.8	0.1	10.6
Establishments of further & higher education(4)	-	0.1	1.3	0.4	3.6	2.0	3.1	0.1	6.0
All establishments	-	0.2	5.9	0.7	14.3	7.5	5.9	0.2	16.6
FEMALES									
Schools(3)									
Public Sector									
Primary	-	0.1	2.1	0.1	1.1	1.0	0.1	-	4.6
Secondary	-	0.2	3.6	0.2	3.3	3.4	0.4	-	4.9
Special	-	-	0.1	-	0.1	0.1	-	-	0.4
Total schools	-	0.3	5.8	0.2	4.4	4.5	0.4	-	9.9
Establishments of further & higher education(4)	-	0.1	0.8	0.1	0.5	0.6	0.2	-	2.4
All establishments	-	0.4	6.6	0.3	4.9	5.1	0.6	0.1	12.3
PERSONS									
Schools(3)									
Public Sector									
Primary	-	0.1	2.5	0.1	1.6	1.3	0.2	-	6.4
Secondary	-	0.3	7.7	0.4	13.4	8.5	3.0	0.1	13.5
Special	-	-	0.2	-	0.2	0.1	-	-	0.7
Total schools	-	0.4	10.4	0.6	15.1	9.9	3.2	0.1	20.5
Establishments of further & higher education(4)	-	0.1	1.3	0.4	3.6	2.0	3.1	0.1	6.0
All establishments									
1989/90	-	0.6	12.4	1.0	19.2	12.6	6.5	0.3	28.9
1988/89	..	..	..	..	..	..	..	..	..
1987/88	..	..	..	..	..	..	..	..	..
1979/80	..	..	..	..	..	..	..	..	..
UNITED KINGDOM									
Universities(5),(6)									
Males	3.1	0.8	2.4	0.5	3.0	2.3	3.5	0.7	3.6
Females	0.6	0.2	0.3	0.1	0.1	0.2	0.1	0.1	0.8
Persons									
1989/90	3.8	1.1	2.7	0.6	3.1	2.5	3.5	0.7	4.4
1988/89	..	..	..	..	..	..	..	..	..
1987/88	..	..	..	..	..	..	..	..	..
1979/80	..	..	..	..	..	..	..	..	..

(1) The subject group of degree is not necessarily the same as the subject taught. University staff are by cost centre and not by degree subject.
(2) Subject headings revised. 1989/90 breakdown not comparable with earlier years.
(3) Information for non-maintained schools is not available.
(4) See paragraph 9.10 of the explanatory notes for graduate shortfall.
(5) Excluding the Open University - 675 professors and lecturers at January 1990.
(6) Full-time teaching and research staff of graduate status paid wholly from general university funds.

TABLE 10[11](continued): Full-time graduate teachers and lecturers by type of establishment, sex and degree subject(1), 1989/90(2)

Thousands

	Business & financial studies	Library & info. science	Languages	Humanities	Creative Arts	Education	Combined General	ALL SUBJECTS
ENGLAND AND WALES								
MALES								
Schools(3)								
Public Sector								
Primary	0.2	-	1.1	1.3	0.6	6.3	1.8	14.5
Secondary	0.8	-	10.5	6.7	3.8	14.7	5.8	73.1
Special	-	-	0.2	0.2	0.1	1.0	0.2	2.3
Total schools	1.0	-	11.8	8.1	4.5	22.0	7.9	90.0
Establishments of further & higher education(4)	1.2	-	2.8	2.0	1.1	1.3	1.1	26.0
All establishments	2.2	0.1	14.6	10.1	5.5	23.3	8.9	116.0
FEMALES								
Schools(3)								
Public Sector								
Primary	0.3	0.2	6.9	4.7	3.2	20.7	3.0	48.0
Secondary	1.4	-	15.4	5.2	3.6	15.1	3.4	59.9
Special	-	-	0.4	0.2	0.2	2.1	0.2	3.9
Total schools	1.8	0.2	22.7	10.1	7.0	37.9	6.6	111.8
Establishments of further & higher education(4)	0.5	-	2.7	0.9	0.5	1.4	0.7	11.5
All establishments	2.3	0.2	25.4	11.1	7.5	39.4	7.3	123.4
PERSONS								
Schools(3)								
Public Sector								
Primary	0.5	0.2	8.0	6.0	3.8	27.1	4.8	62.6
Secondary	2.2	-	25.9	11.8	7.4	29.7	9.2	133.1
Special	0.1	-	0.6	0.4	0.3	3.1	0.5	6.1
Total schools	2.8	0.2	34.5	18.3	11.5	59.9	14.4	201.8
Establishments of further & higher education(4)	1.2	-	2.8	2.0	1.1	1.3	1.1	26.0
All establishments								
1989/90	4.4	0.3	39.9	21.2	13.1	62.7	16.2	239.4
1988/89	..	..	..	..	..	..	..	236.6
1987/88	..	..	..	..	..	..	..	235.6
1979/80	..	..	..	..	..	..	..	188.7
UNITED KINGDOM								
Universities(5),(6)								
Males	-	1.1	2.3	1.8	0.4	1.0	0.2	26.8
Females	-	0.2	0.9	0.3	0.1	0.3	0.1	4.3
Persons								
1989/90	-	1.4	3.2	2.0	0.5	1.3	0.3	31.0
1988/89	..	..	..	..	..	..	..	30.3
1987/88	..	..	..	..	..	..	..	30.0
1979/80	..	..	..	..	..	..	..	33.9

(see previous page for footnotes)

TEACHING STAFF

TABLE 11[10]: Full-time teachers and lecturers by type of establishment, sex and age: average salary summary, 1989/90(1)

Thousands

	Under 25	25-29	30-34	35-39	40-44	45-49	50-54	55-59	60 and over	Total	Average salary(2)
UNITED KINGDOM											
MALES											
Public sector schools											
Primary(3)	1	3	4	8	10	6	4	3	1	38	16,701
Secondary	1	8	16	27	30	19	14	7	2	125	16,759
Special(4)	-	-	1	1	1	1	1	-	-	6	17,901
Total schools(4),(5)	2	11	20	37	42	26	18	10	3	169	16,788
HE/FE establishments(6)	-	2	5	8	14	11	10	7	3	59	18,938
Universities(7)	-	1	3	4	5	5	5	3	1	27	19,460
All establishments(8)	2	14	27	49	61	43	33	19	8	256	15,395
FEMALES											
Public sector schools											
Primary(3)	8	17	16	30	36	26	22	13	3	170	14,484
Secondary	4	14	18	22	22	17	12	5	1	114	15,127
Special(4)	-	1	2	2	3	2	2	1	-	13	15,794
Total schools(4),(5)	12	32	35	54	61	45	35	19	4	297	14,792
HE/FE establishments(6)	-	2	4	5	7	6	4	2	1	30	16,594
Universities(7)	-	-	1	1	1	1	-	-	-	4	15,467
All establishments(8)	12	34	39	60	69	51	40	22	5	332	14,725
PERSONS											
Public sector schools											
Primary(3)	9	19	19	38	46	32	26	16	4	209	14,916
Secondary	5	23	34	49	52	36	25	12	3	239	15,974
Special(4)	-	1	2	4	4	3	2	1	-	19	16,491
Total schools(4),(5)	14	43	55	90	102	71	54	29	7	467	15,525
HE/FE establishments(6)	-	3	8	14	21	17	14	9	4	90	18,227
Universities(7)	-	2	3	4	6	6	5	3	2	31	18,657
All establishments(8)	15	48	67	109	129	94	73	41	13	588	15,024
ENGLAND AND WALES											
Public sector schools(9)											
Males	2	10	17	30	35	22	15	8	3	142	16,776
Females	10	27	28	43	50	37	29	16	3	243	14,785
SCOTLAND											
Public sector schools(9)											
Males	-	1	2	3	4	2	2	1	-	15	..
Females	1	3	4	6	6	4	3	2	1	30	..
NORTHERN IRELAND											
Grant-aided schools(9),(10)											
Males	-	-	1	2	1	1	1	-	-	7	16,080
Females	1	1	2	3	2	1	1	1	-	12	13,967

(1) All data for Scotland has been estimated.

(2) Excluding Scotland.

(3) Including nursery schools.

(4) Excluding independent, and in Scotland grant-aided, special schools.

(5) Data for non-maintained schools are not available by age. Teachers (excluding independent schools in Scotland) numbered 20,000 men and 23,000 women.

(6) Data by age were not available for lecturers in teachers training in Northern Ireland (103 men, 47 women).

(7) Full-time teaching and research staff paid wholly from general university funds. The average salary is that of non-clinical staff.

(8) Excludes 340 men and 316 women in England and Wales whose salary details are not known.

(9) Excluding special schools.

(10) Excludes 156 supply and peripatetic teachers in Northern Ireland.

SCHOOLS

TABLE 12: Full-time and part-time pupils in school, by age(1) and sex: number and as a percentage of the population

(i) Public sector schools

	1965/66	1970/71	1975/76	1980/81	1985/86(2)	1989/90 (3)	1990/91
Number (thousands)							
PERSONS							
2-4(4)	245	351	545	753	872	923	954
5-10	4,665	5,336	5,257	4,555	3,911	4,105	4,136
11	706	789	907	844	682	607	660
12-14	2,092	2,259	2,573	2,591	2,304	1,854	1,817
Total 2-14	7,708	8,734	9,281	8,744	7,769	7,489	7,567
15	414	476	813	877	785	672	637
16	178	226	384	234	242	245	252
17	95	123	140	135	135	158	160
18 and over	37	42	44	15	21	22	25
MALES							
14	354	373	428	447	417	329	316
15	213	244	415	446	400	343	326
16	94	116	194	109	116	117	120
17	52	64	71	66	66	75	76
18 and over	24	25	25	9	11	12	13
FEMALES							
14	339	357	410	429	399	314	301
15	201	232	398	431	385	329	311
16	84	110	189	125	126	128	132
17	43	59	69	69	69	82	84
18 and over	13	17	19	6	9	11	12
UNITED KINGDOM(3)	8,432	9,602	10,662	10,005	8,952	8,586	8,640
ENGLAND	}	7,823	8,714	8,185	7,306	6,992	7,045
	} 7,279						
WALES	}	500	563	532	483	468	469
SCOTLAND	880	966	1,054	970	861	786	787
NORTHERN IRELAND(3)	272	313	332	318	302	339	340
As a percentage of population(5)(6)							
PERSONS							
2-4(4)	8.7	12.5	22.4	38.4	40.4	40.8	41.5
5-10	94.6	95.1	96.4	96.5	95.3	94.2	94.1
11	92.8	93.7	94.1	94.8	94.9	91.8	91.5
12-14	91.8	92.9	92.9	93.8	93.9	92.3	91.9
15	53.1	63.0	92.4	91.1	90.7	92.8	91.7
16	21.8	29.6	45.0	24.2	27.1	31.9	34.7
17	11.0	16.0	16.5	14.3	15.0	19.2	20.7
18 and over(7)	3.9	5.4	5.3	1.6	2.3	2.6	3.0
MALES							
14	91.2	92.7	92.6	92.9	93.0	92.4	91.7
15	53.2	63.1	92.0	90.2	90.1	92.2	91.2
16	22.4	29.7	44.2	21.9	25.4	29.6	32.1
17	11.8	16.4	16.4	13.7	14.3	17.9	19.1
18 and over(7)	4.8	6.4	5.9	1.9	2.4	2.6	3.0
FEMALES							
14	91.5	93.5	93.4	94.0	93.7	93.1	92.5
15	53.0	63.0	92.8	92.2	91.4	93.3	92.2
16	21.0	29.4	45.5	26.6	28.9	34.3	37.4
17	10.1	15.5	16.7	15.0	15.6	20.6	22.4
18 and over(7)	2.9	4.4	4.7	1.3	2.1	2.5	3.0

(1) Age at beginning of January up to and including 1976 and at 31 August for 1980/81 and later years. Age data for Scotland has been adjusted to 31 August for 1980. Age data for Northern Ireland has been adjusted to 31 August for 1980 onwards.

(2) In the 1985/86 column, data for Scotland relate to 1984/85.

(3) Wef 89/90 includes N Ireland voluntary grammar schools formerly allocated to the independent sector.

(4) See section 5 and paragraph 10.2 of the explanatory notes regarding comparisons with other tables.

(5) The Registrars General estimates of total population have sometimes been slightly below the number of children found to have attended school.

(6) See paragraph 6.1 of the explanatory notes.

(7) As a percentage of the 18 years age group.

(8) For non-maintained schools in England, pupils' ages have been estimated.

TABLE 12: Full-time and part-time pupils in school, by age(1) and sex: number and as a percentage of the population

(ii) All schools

	1965/66	1970/71	1975/76	1980/81(8)	1985/86(2)	1989/90 (3)	1990/91
Number (thousands)							
PERSONS							
2-4(4)	269	384	576	792	917	979	1,012
5-10	4,891	5,545	5,453	4,752	4,096	4,312	4,346
11	763	844	965	903	737	658	714
12-14	2,283	2,443	2,768	2,777	2,487	2,011	1,975
Total 2-14	8,206	9,216	9,762	9,224	8,237	7,961	8,046
15	475	534	876	940	845	726	691
16	226	273	432	280	286	289	295
17	128	157	175	168	169	194	197
18 and over	49	53	56	21	28	29	32
MALES							
14	386	404	462	481	452	358	344
15	244	274	449	481	433	373	355
16	120	142	222	136	141	141	144
17	72	84	91	85	86	96	96
18 and over	32	32	32	13	16	16	17
FEMALES							
14	370	386	439	457	428	339	326
15	231	259	427	459	412	354	336
16	106	131	211	144	145	147	151
17	56	73	84	82	84	98	100
18 and over	17	21	24	8	12	14	15
UNITED KINGDOM(3)	9,084	10,232	11,301	10,633	9,565	9,199	9,260
ENGLAND }	} 7,856	8,361	9,258	8,720	7,830	7,557	7,617
WALES }	}	512	576	545	495	480	482
SCOTLAND	921	1,006	1,094	1,005	894	821	821
NORTHERN IRELAND(3)	307	353	374	363	346	340	341
As a percentage of population(5)(6)							
PERSONS							
2-4(4)	9.5	13.7	23.7	40.4	42.6	43.3	44.1
5-10	99.1	98.8	100.0	100.7	99.9	98.9	98.9
11	100.3	100.2	100.1	101.4	102.5	99.6	99.0
12-14	100.2	100.5	100.0	100.5	101.7	100.1	99.8
15	61.0	70.6	99.5	97.7	97.3	100.3	99.5
16	27.7	35.6	50.6	29.0	32.1	37.5	40.6
17	14.8	20.3	20.7	17.8	18.8	23.6	25.5
18 and over(7)	5.1	7.0	6.8	2.3	3.0	3.3	3.8
MALES							
14	99.6	100.6	100.0	100.0	100.6	100.6	99.8
15	61.0	70.9	99.6	97.3	97.4	100.1	99.4
16	28.7	36.3	50.6	27.4	30.9	35.7	38.4
17	16.2	21.3	21.0	17.6	18.5	22.7	24.3
18 and over(7)	6.4	8.3	7.5	2.8	3.3	3.5	3.9
FEMALES							
14	99.9	101.1	100.0	100.2	100.5	100.4	100.0
15	60.9	70.3	99.5	98.1	97.8	100.5	99.6
16	26.7	34.9	50.8	30.6	33.4	39.5	42.8
17	13.2	19.3	20.4	17.8	19.0	24.6	26.8
18 and over(7)	3.7	5.6	6.0	1.8	2.8	3.2	3.7

See footnotes applicable to Table 12(i).

SCHOOLS

TABLE 13: Full-time and part-time pupils by age, sex and school type, 1990/91

Thousands

| Age at 31 August(7) | Public sector schools or departments | | | | | Non-maintained(1) | | | ALL SCHOOLS |
	Nursery	Primary	Secondary (2)	Special schools	Total	Special schools (5)(6)	Other (3)(4)	Total	
MALES									
2 - 4(8)	53.7	430.2	-	4.6	488.5	0.1	29.0	29.1	517.5
5	0.4	361.1	-	2.8	364.3	0.1	15.4	15.5	379.8
6	-	347.4	-	3.1	350.5	0.1	15.2	15.3	365.8
7	-	347.1	-	3.8	350.9	0.1	16.6	16.7	367.6
8	-	341.5	-	4.5	345.9	0.2	18.4	18.6	364.5
9	-	323.4	22.5	5.2	351.1	0.2	20.3	20.5	371.5
10	-	320.5	27.6	6.0	354.1	0.3	22.1	22.4	376.5
11	-	57.6	274.4	6.4	338.4	0.4	28.3	28.7	367.1
12	-	0.6	302.6	6.5	309.7	0.4	27.6	28.0	337.7
13	-	-	297.0	6.9	304.0	0.4	27.5	27.9	331.9
14	-	-	308.5	7.6	316.1	0.5	27.5	28.0	344.2
15	-	-	317.8	7.9	325.7	0.5	28.8	29.3	355.0
16	-	-	117.7	2.4	120.0	0.4	23.1	23.5	143.5
17	-	-	74.3	1.6	75.9	0.3	20.2	20.5	96.4
18	-	-	10.1	1.3	11.4	0.2	3.0	3.2	14.6
19 and over	-	-	1.0	0.1	1.1	0.1	0.8	0.9	2.0
TOTAL	54.0	2,529.4	1,753.6	70.6	4,407.7	4.2	323.8	328.0	4,735.6
FEMALES									
2 - 4(8)	50.6	411.7	-	2.9	465.3	0.1	28.8	28.9	494.2
5	0.2	344.7	-	-	346.5	-	14.6	14.7	361.2
6	-	333.5	-	1.7	335.2	0.1	14.6	14.6	349.8
7	-	330.9	-	2.0	332.9	0.1	15.5	15.6	348.5
8	-	328.2	-	2.4	330.7	0.1	16.9	17.0	347.6
9	-	311.8	21.7	2.7	336.2	0.1	18.4	18.5	354.6
10	-	308.9	26.4	2.9	338.3	0.1	20.0	20.2	358.4
11	-	54.8	263.6	3.2	321.5	0.2	25.1	25.3	346.8
12	-	0.5	292.8	3.2	296.5	0.2	24.4	24.6	321.0
13	-	-	286.3	3.2	289.5	0.2	24.2	24.4	313.9
14	-	-	297.6	3.7	301.3	0.2	24.3	24.5	325.9
15	-	-	307.5	3.8	311.3	0.3	24.7	25.0	336.2
16	-	-	130.4	1.6	132.0	0.2	18.9	19.2	151.1
17	-	-	82.5	1.3	83.8	0.2	16.3	16.5	100.3
18	-	-	9.9	1.0	10.9	0.1	2.2	2.3	13.3
19 and over	-	-	1.0	0.1	1.1	0.1	0.5	0.6	1.7
TOTAL	50.9	2,425.1	1,719.7	37.1	4,232.8	2.2	289.6	291.8	4,524.5
PERSONS									
2 - 4(8)	104.3	841.9	-	7.5	953.7	0.2	57.8	58.0	1,011.7
5	0.6	705.9	-	4.3	710.8	0.1	30.1	30.2	741.0
6	-	680.9	-	4.8	685.7	0.1	29.8	29.9	715.6
7	-	677.9	-	5.8	683.8	0.2	32.1	32.3	716.1
8	-	669.7	-	6.9	676.6	0.3	35.3	35.6	712.1
9	-	635.2	44.1	7.9	687.2	0.3	38.7	38.9	726.2
10	-	629.4	54.1	8.9	692.4	0.4	42.2	42.5	734.9
11	-	112.4	538.0	9.5	659.9	0.6	53.4	54.0	713.9
12	-	1.1	595.4	9.7	606.2	0.5	52.0	52.5	658.7
13	-	-	583.3	10.2	593.5	0.6	51.7	52.3	645.8
14	-	-	606.2	11.3	617.4	0.7	51.8	52.6	670.0
15	-	-	625.3	11.7	637.0	0.8	53.5	54.3	691.3
16	-	-	248.0	4.0	252.0	0.6	42.0	42.6	294.7
17	-	-	156.8	2.8	159.7	0.5	36.5	37.0	196.6
18	-	-	20.0	2.3	22.4	0.3	5.2	5.5	27.9
19 and over	-	-	2.0	0.1	2.2	0.2	1.3	1.6	3.7
TOTAL of which	104.9	4,954.5	3,473.3	107.7	8,640.4	6.4	613.4	619.7	9,260.2
ENGLAND	52.2	4,047.5	2,853.3	91.7	7,044.7	6.0	565.9	572.0	7,616.7
WALES	3.7	276.8	185.2	3.7	469.4	-	12.1	12.1	481.6
SCOTLAND	44.0	440.6	293.7	8.4	786.6	0.3	34.3	34.6	821.3
NORTHERN IRELAND	4.9	189.5	141.1	4.0	339.6	-	1.0	1.0	340.7

(1) See paragraph 2.2 of the explanatory notes.
(2) Wef 1989/90 includes Northern Ireland voluntary grammar schools formerly allocated to the independent sector.
(3) Contains pupils in grant-aided and independent schools in Scotland.
(4) Excludes Northern Ireland voluntary grammar schools allocated to the maintained sector wef 1989/90.
(5) For Scotland grant-aided schools only.
(6) See paragraphs 10.6 to 10.9 (inclusive) of the explanatory notes.
(7) Estimated for Northern Ireland.
(8) See section 5 and paragraph 10.2 of the explanatory notes regarding comparisons with other tables.

TABLE 14: Number of pupils and teachers : pupil/teacher ratios by school type

	1965/66 (1)	1970/71 (1)	1975/76 (1)	1980/81 (1)	1980/81	1985/86	1989/90	1990/91
UNITED KINGDOM								
Pupils (thousands)(2)								
Public sector								
Nursery	31.1	35.2	47.1	55.5	55.5	56.9 (3)	59.4	60.4
Primary	5,151.5	5,882.9	5,940.3	5,087.3	5,087.3	4,520.8	+,747.7	4,812.3
Secondary	3,165.0	3,554.7	4,448.4	4,606.3	4,606.3	4,080.0	3,491.6 (4)	3,473.3
Non-maintained(5)	632.3	605.6	614.6	613.5	629.0	597.1	596.6	603.8
Special	88.0	103.3	149.5	146.7	147.2	130.0	114.6	112.5
All schools	9,067.9	10,181.7	11,199.9	10,509.2	10,525.3	9,384.8 (3)	9,010.0	9,062.3
Teachers (thousands)(2)								
Public sector								
Nursery	1.1	1.3	2.1	2.6	2.6	2.6 (3)	2.7	2.8
Primary	182.8	207.4	249.5	227.8	227.8	205.8	219.0	220.6
Secondary	176.2	199.9	264.1	281.6	281.6	260.5	236.6 (4)	232.3
Non-maintained(5)	45.4	43.3	43.7	46.6	47.9	51.8	54.6	56.3
Special	7.9	9.9	17.1	19.5	19.8	19.6	19.6	19.6
All schools	413.4	461.8	576.5	578.1	579.1	540.3 (3)	532.5	531.6
Pupils per teacher								
Public sector								
Nursery	27.8	26.6	22.1	21.5	21.5	21.7 (3)	21.8	21.5
Primary	28.2	27.1	23.8	22.3	22.3	22.0	21.7	21.8
Secondary	18.0	17.8	16.8	16.4	16.4	15.7	14.8 (4)	15.0
Non-maintained(5)	13.9	14.0	14.1	13.2	13.1	11.5	10.9	10.7
Special	11.1	10.5	8.7	7.5	7.4	6.6	5.8	5.7
All schools	21.9	22.0	19.4	18.2	18.2	17.4 (3)	16.9	17.0
ENGLAND								
Pupils per teacher								
Public sector								
Nursery	24.9	19.1	21.1	19.7	19.7	19.6	19.3	18.9
Primary	28.2	27.0	24.0	22.6	22.6	22.1	21.8	22.0
Secondary	18.3	17.9	17.0	16.6	16.6	15.9	15.0	15.3
Non-maintained	13.8	13.7	13.4	12.5	12.5	11.3	10.9	10.8
Special	11.2	10.2	8.6	7.6	7.6	6.8	5.9	5.8
All schools	21.9	21.4	19.4	18.2	18.2	17.4	17.0	17.2
WALES								
Pupils per teacher								
Public sector								
Nursery	20.7	19.9	19.4	19.0	19.0	20.2	20.8	20.6
Primary	25.0	25.0	22.8	21.7	21.7	22.1	22.3	22.3
Secondary	19.0	18.3	17.1	16.6	16.6	16.1	15.3	15.4
Non-maintained	13.3	13.8	12.3	12.1	12.1	10.7	10.5	9.8
Special	10.9	10.4	10.9	7.7	7.7	7.0	6.5	6.3
All schools	21.7	21.4	19.6	18.5	18.5	18.2	18.1	18.2
SCOTLAND								
Pupils per teacher								
Public sector								
Nursery	..	36.6	24.5	25.3	25.3	..	26.3	25.7
Primary	..	27.9	22.4	20.3	20.3	20.4	19.7	19.5
Secondary	..	16.1	15.1	14.4	14.4	13.5	12.4	12.2
Non-maintained	..	17.3	16.3	15.1	13.0	12.2	10.8	10.6
Special	..	11.6	9.7	6.8	6.2	5.4	4.7	4.5
All schools	..	22.1	18.6	16.9	16.7	..	15.3	15.2
NORTHERN IRELAND								
Pupils per teacher								
All grant-aided schools								
Nursery	24.7	27.6	30.0	23.5	23.5	23.5	24.0	24.7
Primary	29.5	28.9	26.4	23.6	23.6	23.4	23.2	22.9
Secondary(4)(6)	19.8	18.6	17.2	15.2	15.2	14.9	14.9 (4)	14.7
Non-maintained(7)	18.7	17.9	17.4	16.5	16.5	15.8	12.2	11.0
Special	11.4	10.7	9.8	8.4	8.4	8.1	7.1	6.9
All schools	24.7	23.5	21.3	18.9	18.9	18.5	18.3	18.1

(1) Excluding independent schools in Scotland. See paragraph 2.2 of the explanatory notes.
(2) Both pupils and teachers include full-time equivalents of part-time. See paragraph 10.2 of the explanatory notes.
(3) Data on nursery schools for Scotland are for 1984/85.
(4) For 1989/90 pupils and teachers in the preparatory departments of grammar schools in Northern Ireland are included in secondary rather than primary schools.
(5) Excluding Northern Ireland independent schools data in 1980/81.
(6) Including Voluntary grammar schools w.e.f. 1989/90, formerly allocated to the non-maintained sector.
(7) W.e.f. 1989/90 Voluntary grammar schools are allocated to the maintained sector.

SCHOOLS

TABLE 15: Schools, full-time and part-time pupils by size of school or department(1), by school type, 1990/91

(i) Number of schools

	25 and under	26 to 50	51 to 100	101 to 200	201 to 300	301 to 400	401 to 600	601 to 800	801 to 1000	1001 to 1500	1501 and over	Total
UNITED KINGDOM												
Public sector schools												
Nursery	72	529	607	154	2	-	-	-	-	-	-	1,364
Primary	527	1,767	3,182	7,928	6,922	2,659	1,078	65	4	3	-	24,135
Secondary	8	15	25	97	230	360	1,065	1,152	923	847	68	4,790
Non-maintained (2),(3),(4)	209	253	355	722	352	184	192	127	70	41	3	2,508
Special (5)	375	467	687	281	12	2	-	-	-	-	-	1,824
All schools	1,191	3,031	4,856	9,182	7,518	3,205	2,335	1,344	997	891	71	34,621
ENGLAND(6)												
Public sector schools												
Nursery	9	273	259	25	-	-	-	-	-	-	-	566
Primary	175	1,119	2,344	6,617	5,881	2,098	778	34	1	-	-	19,047
Secondary	-	2	10	73	188	282	877	944	766	699	56	3,897
Non-maintained(3)	171	219	312	689	332	168	177	118	67	35	1	2,289
Special	126	382	610	251	9	2	-	-	-	-	-	1,380
All schools	481	1,995	3,535	7,655	6,410	2,550	1,832	1,096	834	734	57	27,179
WALES												
Public sector schools												
Nursery	-	15	33	6	-	-	-	-	-	-	-	54
Primary	58	217	304	577	390	138	31	2	-	-	-	1,717
Secondary	-	-	-	1	3	13	41	64	49	56	3	230
Non-maintained	12	8	9	20	10	5	4	3	-	-	-	71
Special	4	26	23	8	-	-	-	-	-	-	-	61
All schools	74	266	369	612	403	156	76	69	49	56	3	2,133
SCOTLAND												
Public sector schools												
Nursery	58	208	268	123	2	-	-	-	-	-	-	659
Primary	269	274	295	519	505	325	177	8	-	-	-	2,372
Secondary	8	13	11	15	10	31	83	95	78	74	6	424
Non-maintained(4)	21	22	28	12	9	11	11	6	3	6	2	131
Special (5)	242	48	36	10	1	-	-	-	-	-	-	337
All schools	598	565	638	679	527	367	271	109	81	80	8	3,923
NORTHERN IRELAND												
All grant-aided schools(7)												
Nursery	5	33	47	-	-	-	-	-	-	-	-	85
Primary	25	157	239	215	146	98	92	21	3	3	-	999
Secondary(7)	-	-	4	8	29	34	64	49	30	18	3	239
Non-maintained	5	4	6	1	1	-	-	-	-	-	-	17
Special	3	11	18	12	2	-	-	-	-	-	-	46
All schools	38	205	314	236	178	132	156	70	33	21	3	1,386

(1) In this table (apart from the independent sector) schools in Scotland and Northern Ireland with more than one department have been counted once for each department, eg a school with nursery, primary and secondary departments has been counted 3 times.

(2) Including grant-aided nursery, primary and secondary schools/departments and independent schools for England and Scotland.

(3) Includes City Technology Colleges.

(4) Includes all grant-aided schools/departments and independent schools for Scotland.

(5) Education authority schools/departments only for Scotland (see paragraph 10.8 of explanatory notes).

(6) Excludes part-time pupils except in nursery schools, where each part-time pupil is counted as 0.5 in both pupil count and school size.

(7) Includes Voluntary Grammar Schools previously recorded as non-maintained.

TABLE 15 (continued): Schools, full-time and part-time pupils by size of school or department(1), by school type, 1990/91

(ii) Number of pupils   Thousands

	25 and under	26 to 50	51 to 100	101 to 200	201 to 300	301 to 400	401 to 600	601 to 800	801 to 1000	1001 to 1500	1501 and over	Total
UNITED KINGDOM												
Public sector schools												
Nursery	1.3	21.2	41.6	19.3	0.5	-	-	-	-	-	-	83.9
Primary	9.1	67.6	237.2	1,235.5	1,684.6	910.4	494.6	43.4	3.4	3.2	-	4,689.1
Secondary	0.1	0.6	2.0	15.5	59.9	126.8	537.3	805.7	824.1	988.8	112.6	3,473.3
Non-maintained (2),(3),(4)	3.2	9.4	26.4	106.5	86.7	63.9	94.8	87.4	62.2	47.3	6.2	594.1
Special (5)	4.5	18.2	49.0	36.2	2.9	0.6	-	-	-	-	-	111.4
All schools	18.3	116.9	356.3	1,413.0	1,834.5	1,101.8	1,126.7	936.5	889.7	1,039.3	118.9	8,951.7
ENGLAND(6)												
Public sector schools												
Nursery	0.2	10.8	17.2	3.0	-	-	-	-	-	-	-	31.2
Primary	3.4	43.0	175.3	1,036.3	1,429.2	717.3	354.4	22.5	0.8	-	-	3,782.1
Secondary	-	0.1	0.8	11.7	48.7	99.4	442.0	659.3	683.4	815.6	92.4	2,853.3
Non-maintained(3)	2.6	8.1	23.3	101.5	81.8	58.2	87.5	81.0	59.5	40.2	2.5	546.3
Special	1.9	15.0	43.6	32.1	2.2	0.6	-	-	-	-	-	95.4
All schools	8.2	77.0	260.2	1,184.5	1,561.8	875.5	883.8	762.8	743.7	855.7	94.9	7,308.3
WALES												
Public sector schools												
Nursery	-	0.6	2.4	0.7	-	-	-	-	-	-	-	3.7
Primary	1.2	8.2	22.5	88.2	94.1	47.0	14.4	1.3	-	-	-	276.8
Secondary	-	-	-	0.2	0.8	4.5	20.8	44.8	44.3	64.8	4.9	185.2
Non-maintained	0.2	0.3	0.7	3.1	2.5	1.7	1.8	1.9	-	-	-	12.1
Special	0.1	1.0	1.6	1.0	-	-	-	-	-	-	-	3.7
All schools	1.4	10.1	27.2	93.3	97.3	53.2	37.0	48.0	44.3	64.8	4.9	481.6
SCOTLAND												
Public sector schools											-	
Nursery	1.0	8.1	18.8	15.6	0.5	-	-	-	-	-	-	44.0
Primary	4.1	10.3	21.5	80.3	125.1	112.3	81.7	5.3	-	-	-	440.6
Secondary	0.1	0.5	0.8	2.4	2.7	10.9	42.3	67.2	69.9	87.3	9.6	293.7
Non-maintained(4)	0.3	0.8	2.0	1.6	2.2	4.0	5.6	4.5	2.7	7.1	3.8	34.6
Special (5)	2.5	1.8	2.5	1.3	0.2	-	-	-	-	-	-	8.4
All schools	8.0	21.5	45.7	101.2	130.7	127.3	129.5	76.9	72.6	94.4	13.4	821.3
NORTHERN IRELAND												
All grant-aided schools(7)												
Nursery	0.1	1.6	3.2	-	-	-	-	-	-	-	-	4.9
Primary	0.4	6.1	17.9	30.8	36.3	33.8	44.1	14.3	2.6	3.2	-	189.5
Secondary(7)	-	-	0.3	1.3	7.7	12.0	32.2	34.4	26.5	21.1	5.7	141.1
Non-maintained	0.1	0.1	0.4	0.2	0.3	-	-	-	-	-	-	1.0
Special	-	0.4	1.3	1.7	0.5	-	-	-	-	-	-	4.0
All schools	0.6	8.3	23.2	34.0	44.7	45.8	76.3	48.7	29.1	24.3	5.7	340.7

See Table 15(i) for footnotes.

SCHOOLS

TABLE 16: Pupils aged 2 to 4 at 31 December(1),(2) by mode and school type; with age and sex

Thousands

	1965/66	1970/71	1975/76	1980/81	1985/86	1989/90	1990/91 PERSONS 2 - 4	1990/91 MALES 2 and 3	1990/91 MALES 4	1990/91 FEMALES 2 and 3	1990/91 FEMALES 4
UNITED KINGDOM(3)											
Full-time											
Public sector(4)											
Nursery	25.5	19.7	19.7	21.6	18.5	16.5	16.1	5.4	2.9	5.1	2.7
Primary	209.0	263.1	349.5	281.5	305.8	346.5	357.2	12.5	170.1	12.1	162.6
Nursery classes	..	..	..	..	..	37.3	47.5	..	..	..	..
Other classes	..	..	..	..	..	309.2	309.7	..	..	..	..
Non-maintained(5)(6)	21.4	18.6	18.8	19.2	20.4	27.0	28.3	5.1	9.0	5.2	9.0
Special(7)	1.8	1.8	4.2	4.1	4.4	4.1	4.0	1.1	1.3	0.8	0.8
All schools	257.8	303.2	392.1	326.4	349.1	394.1	405.6	24.2	183.3	23.1	175.0
Part-time(8)											
Public sector(4)											
Nursery(9)	9.0	29.1	54.4	67.1	77.2	67.5	68.3	24.5	10.7	23.3	9.9
Primary(9)	-	37.5	116.8	167.1	228.0	286.6	303.3	114.8	40.1	110.5	37.9
Nursery classes(9)	..	..	..	..	..	263.2	275.9	..	..	..	..
Other classes	..	..	..	..	..	23.4	27.5	..	..	..	..
Non-maintained(5)(6)	2.2	14.1	12.1	11.6	14.9	19.1	19.5	8.5	1.2	8.7	1.2
Special(7)	-	0.1	0.6	1.0	1.5	2.2	2.4	1.2	0.3	0.7	0.2
All schools	11.2	80.8	183.9	246.9	321.6	375.4	393.6	148.9	52.2	143.2	49.2
All full-time and part-time pupils aged 2 - 4 years	269.0	384.0	576.0	573.3	670.7	769.5	799.1	173.1	235.5	166.4	224.2
ENGLAND											
All full-time	{	248.9	319.5	259.4	281.0	313.6	325.7	18.5	148.0	17.8	141.4
All part-time	{	69.8	153.9	202.2	265.9	312.6	328.8	131.7	36.3	126.5	34.3
	237.9 {										
WALES(2)	11.2 {										
All full-time	{	29.6	38.0	30.4	31.4	44.4	44.4	3.8	19.1	3.6	17.9
All part-time	{	2.6	10.5	14.1	18.2	20.7	21.1	10.4	0.3	10.0	0.3
SCOTLAND(10)											
All full-time	{	6.9	12.0	14.8	..	14.2	14.1	0.6	6.5	0.7	6.3
	9.2 {										
All part-time	{	8.4	19.5	28.8	..	39.2	40.7	5.9	15.0	5.8	14.0
NORTHERN IRELAND											
All full-time(11)	10.7	17.7	22.6	21.8	22.1	21.9	21.4	1.2	9.7	1.1	9.4
All part-time	-	-	-	1.7	2.5	2.9	3.1	0.9	0.7	0.9	0.5

(1) See section 5 of the explanatory notes. Age detail for England has been estimated.

(2) August-based ages for special and independent schools in Wales, up to 1989/90. From 1990/91, August-based ages for all schools in Wales.

(3) In the 1985/86 column, data for Scotland relate to 1984/85.

(4) Grant-aided schools for Northern Ireland.

(5) Includes grant-aided nursery and primary schools/depts and independent schools for Scotland for 89/90.

(6) From 1990/91 includes all grant-aided schools/departments and independent schools for Scotland.

(7) From 1990/91 Education Authority Schools only in Scotland.

(8) Each part-time pupil has been counted as one.

(9) Prior to 1988/89, pupils in nursery classes within primary schools in Scotland are included in the nursery school figures. In 1988/89 such pupils in Scotland numbered 16,924.

(10) See paragraph 10.2 of the explanatory notes.

(11) Including pupils in all grant-aided schools and independent schools in Northern Ireland.

TABLE 17: Pupils with special needs

(i) Numbers of public sector and assisted special schools(1), full-time pupils and teachers

			1965/66	1970/71	1975/76	1980/81	1985/86	1989/90	1990/91
Hospital schools									
Schools									
Public sector(2)			81	77	152	132	89	52	48
Assisted			10	9	7	4	2	-	-
Total			91	86	159	136	91	52	48
of which:	England	}	91	82	151	131	87	50	47
	Wales	}		4	8	5	4	2	1
	Northern Ireland(2)		-	-	-	-	-	-	-
Full-time pupils (thousands)(2)			4.1	3.6	9.5	7.1	4.4	1.4	0.9
Full-time teachers (thousands)(2)			0.5	0.5	1.2	1.2	0.7	0.4	0.4
Other special schools or departments(3)									
Schools									
Public sector			831	996	1,627	1,763	1,726	1,712	1,695
Assisted			126	117	120	112	95	89	87
Day			577	703	1,276	1,412	1,464	1,540	1,522
Boarding			380	410	471	463	357	261	260
Total			957	1,113	1,747	1,875	1,821	1,801	1,782
of which:	England	}	811	901	1,394	1,462	1,406	1,348	1,333
	Wales	}		32	66	68	63	61	60
	Scotland(3)		129	159	264	319	328	346	343
	Northern Ireland(4)		17	21	23	26	24	46	46
Full-time pupils (thousands)(3),(5)			83.7	99.5	139.5	139.2	126.0	112.1	110.8
of which:	England	}	72.4	84.3	119.8	120.3	107.7	95.8	94.5
	Wales	}		2.5	4.3	4.6	4.1	3.6	3.6
	Scotland(3)		9.7	10.6	13.1	11.8	11.7	8.8	8.7
	Northern Ireland(4)		1.6	2.1	2.3	2.5	2.6	3.9	4.0
Full-time and FTE of part-time Teachers (thousands)(3)			7.4	9.3	15.8	18.4	18.5	19.0	19.1

(1) See paragraphs 10.6 to 10.9 (inclusive) of the explanatory notes.

(2) Revised data for Northern Ireland. Units attached to Hospital Schools are excluded from the table.

(3) Includes all scottish special schools. In the 1985/86 column, data for Scotland relate to 1984/85.

(4) Figures from 1987 onwards include schools and pupils which were previously the responsibilty of the Northern Ireland Department of Health and Social Security, which were formerly excluded - 22 schools and 1,333 pupils in 1987/88.

(5) See paragraph 10.9 of the explanatory notes.

(ii) Pupils with statements of special needs in other public sector schools

Thousands

		1985/86	1986/87	1987/88	1988/89	1989/90	1990/91	
Public sector primary schools(6)		22.8 (7)	24.0	28.5	31.8	35.0	40.3	(8)
Public sector secondary schools(6)		15.4 (7)	17.4	21.8	25.7	29.4	34.8	(9)
Total United Kingdom		38.2	41.3	50.2	57.4	64.4	75.2	
of which:	England	30.0	33.3	40.9	47.3	54.3	62.0	
	Wales	5.8	6.0	7.5	7.5	7.1	8.9	
	Scotland	0.7	0.7	0.8	1.1	1.3	2.3	
	Northern Ireland	1.7	1.3	1.1	1.6	1.7	2.0	

(6) Including middle schools deemed primary or secondary as appropriate.

(7) Including estimated primary/secondary split for Wales.

(8) For Northern Ireland includes preparatory departments of grammar schools.

(9) For Northern Ireland includes secondary departments of grammar schools.

SCHOOLS

TABLE 18: Pupils in public sector secondary education by school type and country

	1965/66 Persons		1970/71 Persons		1975/76 Persons		1980/81 Persons		1985/86 Persons		1989/90 Persons		1990/91 Persons	
	000s	%	000s	%	000s	%	000s	%	000s	%	000s	%	000s	%
ENGLAND														
Maintained secondary schools														
Middle deemed secondary	-	-	55	1.9	223	6.0	268	7.0	224	6.6	186	6.5	182	6.4
Modern	1,454	55.1	1,121	38.0	574	15.5	229	6.0	143	4.2	108	3.8	94	3.3
Grammar	660	25.0	544	18.4	285	7.7	131	3.4	103	3.0	98	3.4	102	3.6
Technical	73	2.8	38	1.3	15	0.4	10	0.3	2	0.1	2	0.1	2	0.1
Comprehensive	262	9.9	1,017	34.4	2,544	68.8	3,168	82.5	2,894	85.4	2,458	85.9	2,446	85.7
Other	189	7.2	178	6.0	60	1.6	34	0.9	22	0.7	10	0.3	28	1.0
Total pupils	2,639	100.0	2,953	100.0	3,700	100.0	3,840	100.0	3,389	100.0	2,863	100.0	2,853	100.0
WALES														
Maintained secondary schools														
Middle deemed secondary	-	-	-	0.1	-	-	-	0.1	-	0.1	-	-	-	-
Modern	70	39.3	43	22.3	16	6.8	4	1.8	1	0.6	-	-	-	-
Grammar	53	29.5	29	15.4	10	4.3	3	1.3	1	0.5	-	-	-	-
Comprehensive	50	28.3	112	58.5	208	88.5	231	96.6	215	98.5	184	99.2	184	99.2
Other	5	2.7	7	3.7	1	0.4	1	0.3	1	0.3	1	0.8	1	0.8
Technical	-	0.2	-	-	-	-	-	-	-	-	-	-	-	-
Total pupils	178	100.0	191	100.0	235	100.0	240	100.0	218	100.0	186	100.0	185	100.0
SCOTLAND														
Public sector secondary schools														
Selective	..	..	89	28.3	4	1.1	1	0.1	..	..	-	-	-	-
Comprehensive	..	..	184	58.7	349	87.6	392	96.0	..	..	299	100.0	294	100.0
Part comprehensive/ part selective	..	..	41	13.0	45	11.3	16	3.8	..	..	-	-	-	-
Total pupils	271	..	314	100.0	398	100.0	408	100.0	361	100.0	299	100.0	294	100.0
NORTHERN IRELAND														
All grant-aided secondary schools														
Secondary intermediate	37	73.5	84	87.7	103	89.3	105	88.6	99	88.2	88	62.3	87	61.4
Grammar(1)	10	20.0	11	11.8	12	10.7	14	11.4	13	11.8	53	37.7	54	38.6
Technical intermediate(2)	3	6.5	-	0.5	-	-	-	-	-	-	-	-	-	-
Total pupils	51	100.0	96	100.0	115	100.0	119	100.0	113	100.0	141	100.0	141	100.0

(1) Includes Voluntary grammar schools w.e.f. 89/90, formerly allocated to the independent sector.

(2) The last of these schools closed in June 1974.

TABLE 19: Pupils leaving school having attempted GCSE/GCE/CSE, by subject

	ENGLAND AND WALES					GREAT BRITAIN				
	1970/71	1975/76	1980/81	1984/85	1985/86	1989/90(1)	1990/91(1)			
			Persons			Persons	Persons	Males	Females	Persons
										(000's)
Percentage attempting:										
English	54.6	77.7	84.2	85.9	85.4	87.5	88.6	86.7	90.5	564.5
Mathematics	49.1	69.4	79.9	81.6	81.0	82.0	83.1	82.1	84.2	529.7
Science	38.4	52.5	62.6	66.1	65.1	78.5	81.0	80.5	81.6	516.5
Technology	22.2	35.4	37.3	38.7	39.1	34.9	35.6	52.4	18.1	227.0
Modern languages	29.0	34.2	37.2	40.2	40.0	48.2	54.1	46.4	62.3	345.0
History and/or Geography	43.1	55.6	61.2	61.9	61.4	60.6	62.0	63.4	60.5	394.9
Creative Arts	20.2	30.9	31.9	32.5	32.5	39.6	41.9	37.0	47.1	266.9
English and Mathematics	48.5	67.0	77.6	79.1	78.3	79.8	81.5	80.0	83.0	519.0
English, Maths and Science	35.0	47.6	59.1	62.5	61.4	74.6	77.2	76.1	78.5	492.1
English, Maths, Science and Modern Languages	21.3	26.2	30.9	34.1	33.7	44.3	50.1	43.3	57.1	319.0
ALL LEAVERS (thousands)	613.4	707.4	777.9	780.6	761.4	681.7	637.2	326.1	311.1	637.2

(1) Due to changes in subject classification from 1988/89, direct comparisons of individual subjects with earlier years are not possible .

POST-COMPULSORY EDUCATION

TABLE 20: Pupils leaving school by age (1) and sex

	During the academic year						Thousands
	1965/66	1970/71	1975/76	1980/81(2)	1985/86	1989/90	1990/91
AGE (1)							
MALES							
14	131	101	.	2	2	2	2
15	123	126	208	311	297	225	201
16	47	56	125	46	58	44	46
17	40	54	60	71	73	81	79
18 and over	32	31	30	11	14	11	11
Total	373	368	423	442	444	362	338
FEMALES							
14	126	100	.	2	2	1	1
15	123	121	197	286	277	200	179
16	48	55	122	57	64	48	49
17	38	53	59	72	73	85	84
18 and over	17	20	22	7	11	10	10
Total	352	349	400	423	427	344	323
PERSONS							
14	257	200	.	4	4	3	3
15	246	248	405	597	573	426	380
16	95	111	247	103	122	93	95
17	79	107	119	143	146	166	162
18 and over	49	50	52	18	25	20	21
TOTALS:							
UNITED KINGDOM	725	717	823	865	871	706	661
ENGLAND	}	577	667	734	718	578	542
	} 623						
WALES	}	36	47	44	43	36	33
SCOTLAND	79	79	91	87	83	68	62
NORTHERN IRELAND	23	24	25	..	27	25	24

(1) Age at beginning of January up to and including 1976 and at previous 31 August for 1981, and later years. See explanatory note 5.1.
(2) Great Britain only.

TABLE 21: Educational and economic activities of 16 - 18 year olds(1)

GREAT BRITAIN

(i) January 1990

AGE	16			17			18			16 - 18		
	Males	Females	Persons	Males	Females	Persons	Males	Females	Persons	Males	Females	Persons
Population (thousands)(2)	382	360	743	407	387	794	434	416	850	1,223	1,163	2,386
Percentage of age group												
In full-time education	48	58	52	35	41	38	21	21	21	34	39	36
School	33	37	35	22	23	23	3	3	3	19	20	19
Further education(3)	14	21	17	12	17	14	7	8	8	11	15	13
Higher education(3)	-	-	-	1	1	1	11	11	11	4	4	4
On YTS (4)	27	18	23	26	16	21	3	1	2	18	11	15
Other(5)	25	24	25	40	43	41	77	77	77	48	49	49
Of which in part-time day education (included in employed/unemployed)(6)	7	3	5	9	4	7	13	5	9	10	4	7

(ii) January 1976 - 1989

AGE	16 - 18											
	January 1976			January 1981			January 1986			January 1989		
	Males	Females	Persons	Males	Females	Persons	Males	Females	Persons	Males	Females	Persons
Population (thousands)(2)	1,231	1,178	2,409	1,405	1,343	2,748	1,349	1,284	2,633	1,270	1,210	2,480
Percentage of age group												
In full-time education												
School	16	16	16	16	17	16	17	17	17	18	19	18
Further education(3)	7	9	8	7	11	9	8	13	11	10	14	12
Higher education(3)	3	3	3	3	3	3	4	3	3	4	4	4
On YTS(7)	-	-	-	5	5	5	12	9	10	19	12	16
Other												
Unemployed(8), (9)	9	7	8	14	12	13	17	13	15	}		
										} 50	51	50
Mainly those in employment (outside YTS)(10)	65	66	65	54	52	53	42	44	43	}		
Of which in part-time day education (included in employed/unemployed)(6)	22	5	14	19	5	13	12	5	8	10	4	7

(1) Age as at 31 August of the preceding year.

(2) Some 6 per cent of the age group 16-18 attended evening only courses in 1990. These cannot be classified by education/employment status and are not shown separately in this table. See Table 22.

(3) Full-time and sandwich excluding private education outside school. Excludes those on full-time YTS within colleges.

(4) Including those in further education establishments attending YTS courses.

(5) Including unemployed and those mainly in employment (outside YTS). See also footnotes (8), (9) & (10).

(6) Public sector part-time day study only, excluding those attending YTS courses. In addition, DFE estimate of employer provision outside Local Education Authority colleges or YTS is 4% of 16 year olds and 6% of 16-18 year olds in 1983-84.(source: Department of Employment:New Entrant Survey). The majority of part-time day students are in employment but some are receiving unemployment benefit under "21 hour rule".

(7) Including those on YOP in 1976 and 1981 and those in further education establishments attending YTS/YOP courses.

(8) Registered unemployed in 1976 and 1981 and claimant unemployed from 1986 (DFE estimates).

(9) In September 1988 16-17 year olds became ineligible for income support and are therefore excluded from the unemployment category from 1988/89.

(10) Residual obtained by subtraction thus reflecting any net error in the other estimates. Including in 1976 and 1981 the unregistered unemployed and those who were neither employed nor seeking work (eg because of domestic responsibilities) and from 1986 those who are seeking work but not claiming benefit and those who are neither employed nor seeking work.

TABLE 22: Numbers and percentages continuing their education aged 16 and over, by age, sex and type of course, 1990/91.

				(i) PERSONS			Home students	
				Age at 31 August 1990				
				Total			25 and	All
	16	17	18	16-18	19-20	21-24	over	Ages
NUMBERS (Thousands)								
Total population	726	771	822	2,319	1,752	3,670	.	.
FULL-TIME AND SANDWICH STUDENTS								
Schools	295	197	28	519	4	-	-	523
Further education	154	129	71	354	38	24	56	472
Higher education	1	9	102	112	265	182	107	667
Universities	-	5	53	57	134	83	37	312
Undergraduates	-	5	53	57	134	62	20	273
Postgraduates	-	-	-	-	-	22	16	39
Polytechnics and other HE estabs	-	4	50	54	131	99	70	356
Undergraduates	-	4	50	54	131	91	62	339
Postgraduates	-	-	-	-	1	7	8	16
Total full-time and sandwich students	449	334	202	985	307	206	163	1,663
PART-TIME STUDENTS								
Further education	143	141	121	405	213	476	2,035	3,134
Day students	98	104	77	280	102	176	783	1,343
Adult education centres(1)	8	2	4	14	31	110	399	555
Other	90	102	74	265	71	65	384	788
Evening only students	45	37	44	125	111	300	1,252	1,791
Adult education centres(1)	27	14	16	57	58	203	707	1,026
Other	18	23	28	68	52	97	545	766
Higher education(2)	-	1	10	11	36	71	291	410
Universities	-	-	-	-	1	6	45	51
Undergraduates	-	-	-	-	1	2	8	11
Postgraduates	-	-	-	-	-	4	37	41
Polytechnics and other HE estabs	-	1	9	11	35	61	156	264
Undergraduates	-	1	9	11	35	58	128	233
Postgraduates	-	-	-	-	-	3	28	31
Open University	-	-	-	-	-	4	90	95
Total part-time students	144	142	131	416	249	546	2,326	3,545
All full-time and part-time students	593	476	332	1,401	555	752	2,490	5,207
AS PERCENTAGE OF THE POPULATION								
FULL-TIME AND SANDWICH STUDENTS								
Schools	40.6	25.5	3.4	22.4	0.2	-	..	..
Further education	21.2	16.7	8.7	15.3	2.1	0.7	..	..
Higher education	0.1	1.1	12.5	4.8	15.1	5.0	..	..
Universities	-	0.6	6.4	2.5	7.7	2.3	..	..
Undergraduates	-	0.6	6.4	2.5	7.6	1.7	..	..
Postgraduates	-	-	-	-	-	0.6	..	..
Polytechnics and other HE estabs	0.1	0.5	6.1	2.3	7.5	2.7	..	..
Undergraduates	0.1	0.5	6.0	2.3	7.5	2.5	..	..
Postgraduates	-	-	-	-	-	0.2	..	..
Total full-time and sandwich students	61.9	43.3	24.5	42.5	17.5	5.6	..	..
PART-TIME STUDENTS								
Further education	19.7	18.2	14.7	17.5	12.1	13.0	..	..
Day students	13.6	13.5	9.4	12.1	5.8	4.8	..	..
Adult education centres(1)	1.1	0.3	0.4	0.6	1.8	3.0	..	..
Other	12.4	13.2	9.0	11.4	4.0	1.8	..	..
Evening only students	6.2	4.8	5.3	5.4	6.3	8.2	..	..
Adult education centres(1)	3.7	1.8	2.0	2.5	3.3	5.5	..	..
Other	2.5	3.0	3.3	2.9	3.0	2.6	..	..
Higher education(2)	-	0.2	1.2	0.5	2.1	1.9	..	..
Universities	-	-	-	-	-	0.2	..	..
Undergraduates	-	-	-	-	-	-	..	..
Postgraduates	-	-	-	-	-	0.1	..	..
Polytechnics and other HE estabs	-	0.2	1.1	0.5	2.0	1.7	..	..
Undergraduates	-	0.2	1.1	0.5	2.0	1.6	..	..
Postgraduates	-	-	-	-	-	0.1	..	..
Open University	-	-	-	-	-	0.1	..	..
Total part-time students	19.8	18.4	15.9	17.9	14.2	14.9	..	..
All full-time and part-time students	81.7	61.7	40.4	60.4	31.7	20.5	..	..

(1) Including estimated age detail for 1,580,600 students aged 16 years or more in adult education centres; excluding youth clubs and centres, 77,000 in 1984/85 (England). Excluding some 605,693 students on courses run by responsible bodies (see explanatory notes 12.8) for whom age detail was not available.

(2) Excluding 81,700 (provisional) students enrolled on nursing and paramedical courses at Department of Health establishments.

TABLE 22: Numbers and percentages continuing their education aged 16 and over, by age, sex and type of course, 1990/91.

				(ii) MALES			Home students	
				Age at 31 August 1990				
				Total			25 and	All
	16	17	18	16-18	19-20	21-24	over	Ages
NUMBERS (Thousands)								
Total population	373	397	422	1,192	895	1,868	.	.
FULL-TIME AND SANDWICH STUDENTS								
Schools	144	96	15	255	2	-	-	257
Further education	71	57	34	162	19	12	21	215
Higher education	-	4	52	57	137	101	50	345
Universities	-	2	29	31	74	48	19	172
Undergraduates	-	2	29	31	74	35	10	149
Postgraduates	-	-	-	-	-	13	9	22
Polytechnics and other HE estabs	-	2	23	25	63	52	32	173
Undergraduates	-	2	23	25	63	49	28	165
Postgraduates	-	-	-	-	-	3	4	8
Total full-time and sandwich students	214	158	101	473	159	112	72	816
PART-TIME STUDENTS								
Further education	79	86	74	238	100	168	593	1,100
Day students	62	72	58	192	58	60	196	507
Adult education centres(1)	3	1	1	5	8	26	70	109
Other	59	72	56	187	50	34	126	398
Evening only students	17	13	16	46	42	108	397	592
Adult education centres(1)	10	5	6	20	22	70	193	305
Other	7	9	11	26	20	37	203	287
Higher education(2)	-	1	7	8	26	43	155	232
Universities	-	-	-	-	-	3	24	28
Undergraduates	-	-	-	-	-	1	3	5
Postgraduates	-	-	-	-	-	2	21	23
Polytechnics and other HE estabs	-	1	7	8	26	38	83	154
Undergraduates	-	1	7	8	26	37	67	137
Postgraduates	-	-	-	-	-	1	16	18
Open University	-	1	21	22	204	2,084	47,016	49,326
Total part-time students	79	86	80	246	126	211	747	1,331
All full-time and part-time students	294	244	181	719	285	323	819	2,147
AS PERCENTAGE OF THE POPULATION								
FULL-TIME AND SANDWICH STUDENTS								
Schools	38.4	24.3	3.5	21.4	0.2	-	..	..
Further education	18.9	14.4	8.1	13.6	2.1	0.6	..	..
Higher education	0.1	1.0	12.3	4.7	15.4	5.4	..	..
Universities	-	0.6	6.8	2.6	8.3	2.6	..	..
Undergraduates	-	0.6	6.8	2.6	8.3	1.9	..	..
Postgraduates	-	-	-	-	-	0.7	..	..
Polytechnics and other HE estabs	0.1	0.5	5.6	2.1	7.1	2.8	..	..
Undergraduates	0.1	0.5	5.5	2.1	7.1	2.6	..	..
Postgraduates	-	-	-	-	-	0.2	..	..
Total full-time and sandwich students	57.5	39.8	23.9	39.7	17.7	6.0	..	..
PART-TIME STUDENTS								
Further education	21.2	21.6	17.5	20.0	11.2	9.0	..	..
Day students	16.7	18.3	13.6	16.1	6.5	3.2	..	..
Adult education centres(1)	0.8	0.2	0.3	0.4	0.9	1.4	..	..
Other	15.9	18.0	13.4	15.7	5.6	1.8	..	..
Evening only students	4.4	3.3	3.8	3.9	4.7	5.8	..	..
Adult education centres(1)	2.6	1.2	1.3	1.7	2.5	3.8	..	..
Other	1.8	2.2	2.5	2.2	2.2	2.0	..	..
Higher education(2)	-	0.2	1.6	0.6	2.9	2.3	..	..
Universities	-	-	-	-	-	0.2	..	..
Undergraduates	-	-	-	-	-	-	..	..
Postgraduates	-	-	-	-	-	0.1	..	..
Polytechnics and other HE estabs	-	0.2	1.6	0.6	2.9	2.0	..	..
Undergraduates	-	0.2	1.6	0.6	2.9	2.0	..	..
Postgraduates	-	-	-	-	-	0.1	..	..
Open University	-	-	-	-	-	0.1	..	..
Total part-time students	21.2	21.8	19.1	20.6	14.1	11.3	..	..
All full-time and part-time students	78.7	61.5	43.0	60.3	31.8	17.3	..	..

See footnotes to Table 22(i)

TABLE 22: Numbers and percentages continuing their education aged 16 and over, by age, sex and type of course, 1990/91.

				(iii) FEMALES				Home students
				Age at 31 August 1990				
				Total			25 and	All
	16	17	18	16-18	19-20	21-24	over	Ages
NUMBERS (Thousands)								
Total population	353	374	400	1,127	857	1,802	.	.
FULL-TIME AND SANDWICH STUDENTS								
Schools	151	100	13	265	2	-	-	266
Further education	83	72	37	192	18	12	35	257
Higher education	-	4	50	55	128	81	57	321
Universities	-	2	24	26	60	35	18	140
Undergraduates	-	2	24	26	60	27	11	124
Postgraduates	-	-	-	-	-	9	8	16
Polytechnics and other HE estabs	-	2	26	29	68	46	39	181
Undergraduates	-	2	26	29	67	42	35	173
Postgraduates	-	-	-	-	-	4	4	9
Total full-time and sandwich students	235	176	101	512	148	94	92	845
PART-TIME STUDENTS								
Further education	64	55	47	167	112	308	1,442	2,030
Day students	36	32	20	87	44	116	587	834
Adult education centres(1)	5	2	2	9	23	85	329	446
Other	31	30	17	78	21	31	258	388
Evening only students	28	23	28	79	68	192	856	1,196
Adult education centres(1)	17	9	11	37	36	133	514	720
Other	11	14	17	42	32	60	341	476
Higher education(2)	-	-	3	3	10	27	137	177
Universities	-	-	-	-	-	2	21	24
Undergraduates	-	-	-	-	-	1	5	6
Postgraduates	-	-	-	-	-	2	16	17
Polytechnics and other HE estabs	-	-	3	3	9	23	73	108
Undergraduates	-	-	3	3	9	21	61	95
Postgraduates	-	-	-	-	-	1	12	13
Open University	-	-	-	-	-	2	43	46
Total part-time students	64	55	50	170	122	335	1,579	2,207
All full-time and part-time students	299	232	151	682	270	429	1,671	3,052
AS PERCENTAGE OF POPULATION								
FULL-TIME AND SANDWICH STUDENTS								
Schools	42.9	26.8	3.3	23.5	0.2	-	..	..
Further education	23.6	19.1	9.3	17.0	2.2	0.7	..	..
Higher education	0.1	1.2	12.6	4.9	14.9	4.5	..	..
Universities	-	0.6	6.0	2.3	7.0	2.0	..	..
Undergraduates	-	0.6	6.0	2.3	7.0	1.5	..	..
Postgraduates	-	-	-	-	-	0.5	..	..
Polytechnics and other HE estabs	0.1	0.6	6.6	2.6	7.9	2.6	..	..
Undergraduates	0.1	0.6	6.6	2.5	7.9	2.3	..	..
Postgraduates	-	-	-	-	0.1	0.2	..	..
Total full-time and sandwich students	66.5	47.1	25.2	45.4	17.3	5.2	..	..
PART-TIME STUDENTS								
Further education	18.2	14.7	11.8	14.8	13.1	17.1	..	..
Day students	10.2	8.4	4.9	7.7	5.1	6.4	..	..
Adult education centres(1)	1.4	0.4	0.6	0.8	2.7	4.7	..	..
Other	8.8	8.0	4.3	6.9	2.4	1.7	..	..
Evening only students	8.0	6.3	6.9	7.0	8.0	10.7	..	..
Adult education centres(1)	4.9	2.4	2.7	3.3	4.2	7.4	..	..
Other	3.1	3.9	4.2	3.8	3.8	3.3	..	..
Higher education(2)	-	0.1	0.7	0.3	1.2	1.5	..	..
Universities	-	-	-	-	-	0.1	..	..
Undergraduates	-	-	-	-	-	-	..	..
Postgraduates	-	-	-	-	-	0.1	..	..
Polytechnics and other HE estabs	-	0.1	0.7	0.3	1.1	1.3	..	..
Undergraduates	-	0.1	0.7	0.3	1.1	1.2	..	..
Postgraduates	-	-	-	-	-	0.1	..	..
Open University	-	-	-	-	-	0.1	..	..
Total part-time students	18.3	14.8	12.5	15.1	14.3	18.6	..	..
All full-time and part-time students	84.8	61.9	37.7	60.5	31.5	23.8	..	..

See footnotes to Table 22(i)

TABLE 23:   Participation rates of pupils and students(1), (2) by sex, age and type of education

Home students   Percentages of the population age group

	1980/81		1985/86		1989/90		1990/91	
Age at 31 August(3)	Full-time	Part-time	Full-time	Part-time	Full-time	Part-time	Full-time	Part-time
MALES								
Schools								
16 - 18	}	-	17.2	-	19.8	-	21.4	-
	} 16.0							
19 - 20	}	-	0.2	-	0.2	-	0.2	-
Further education(4)								
16 - 18(5)	7.2	26.7	9.8	21.2	12.5	21.5	13.6	20.0
19 - 20	1.4	14.2	1.5	11.4	1.8	11.4	2.1	11.2
21 - 24	0.5	8.5	0.4	8.6	0.5	9.0	0.6	9.0
Higher education								
16 - 18	3.5	0.8	3.5	0.6	4.3	0.7	4.7	0.6
19 - 20	12.3	3.6	12.9	3.1	14.1	3.1	15.4	2.9
21 - 24	4.7	2.8	4.6	2.4	5.0	2.3	5.4	2.3
Total								
16 - 18(5)	26.7	27.5	30.5	21.9	36.5	22.2	39.7	20.6
19 - 20	13.8	17.8	14.6	14.5	16.2	14.5	17.7	14.1
21 - 24	5.2	11.3	5.0	11.1	5.5	11.4	6.0	11.3
FEMALES								
Schools								
16 - 18	}	-	18.1	-	21.4	-	23.5	-
	} 16.9							
19 - 20	}	-	0.2	-	0.2	-	0.2	-
Further education(4)								
16 - 18(5)	11.1	17.0	13.6	18.6	15.4	16.6	17.0	14.8
19 - 20	1.3	11.2	1.6	12.4	1.9	13.2	2.2	13.1
21 - 24	0.5	14.9	0.5	15.6	0.6	16.7	0.7	17.1
Higher education								
16 - 18	3.0	0.2	3.2	0.2	4.3	0.3	4.9	0.3
19 - 20	9.8	0.9	11.4	1.0	13.3	1.2	14.9	1.2
21 - 24	2.9	1.0	3.4	1.1	4.1	1.5	4.5	1.5
Total								
16 - 18(5)	31.2	17.2	34.9	18.8	41.1	16.8	45.4	15.1
19 - 20	11.0	12.1	13.1	13.4	15.4	14.4	17.3	14.3
21 - 24	3.4	15.9	3.9	16.7	4.7	18.1	5.2	18.6
PERSONS								
Schools								
16 - 18	}	-	17.7	-	20.6	-	22.4	-
	} 16.5							
19 - 20	}	-	0.2	-	0.2	-	0.2	-
Further education(4)								
16 - 18(5)	9.2	22.0	11.6	20.0	13.9	19.1	15.3	17.5
19 - 20	1.3	12.7	1.5	11.9	1.8	12.2	2.1	12.1
21 - 24	0.5	11.7	0.5	12.1	0.5	12.8	0.7	13.0
Higher education								
16 - 18	3.3	0.5	3.4	0.4	4.3	0.5	4.8	0.5
19 - 20	11.0	2.3	12.2	2.0	13.7	2.2	15.1	2.1
21 - 24	3.8	1.9	4.0	1.8	4.6	1.9	5.0	1.9
Total								
16 - 18(5)	28.9	22.5	32.7	20.4	38.8	19.6	42.5	17.9
19 - 20	12.4	15.0	13.9	14.0	15.8	14.4	17.5	14.2
21 - 24	4.3	13.6	4.5	13.8	5.1	14.7	5.6	14.9

(1) Full-time includes sandwich course students.
(2) Part-time includes evening students.
(3) See paragraph 5.1 of the explanatory notes.
(4) Including estimated age detail for 473 thousand students aged under 25 in adult education centres in 1990/91.
(5) Including under-16s in Scotland for 1980/81.

FURTHER AND HIGHER EDUCATION

TABLE 24 [26]: Students enrolled on further education courses leading to specified qualifications by age, sex and mode of attendance

	BTEC (1) SCOTVEC (2)	Royal Society of Arts	City and Guilds	GCSE GCE CSE SCE	Other specified courses	ALL COURSES LEADING TO SPECIFIED QUALIFICATIONS				
						United Kingdom	England	Wales	Scotland	Northern Ireland (3)
Age at 31 August 1990										
STUDENTS AGED 16-18										
Full-time and sandwich										
Males	72.8	0.5	22.7	46.7	9.5	152.1	128.8	8.4	9.0	5.8
Females	67.3	8.6	22.8	57.3	28.8	184.9	157.8	10.5	9.4	7.1
Persons	140.0	9.1	45.5	104.0	38.3	336.9	286.6	18.9	18.4	12.9
Part-time day										
Males	57.7	1.3	112.6	8.2	7.3	187.1	150.0	8.1	21.4	7.6
Females	25.2	8.4	23.2	10.4	7.9	75.2	57.5	2.3	11.1	4.3
Persons	82.9	9.8	135.8	18.7	15.2	262.3	207.5	10.4	32.5	11.8
Evening only										
Males	3.1	0.5	6.7	19.4	3.2	33.0	28.5	1.1	2.3	1.2
Females	2.4	9.9	2.5	28.5	5.0	48.3	39.9	2.0	4.2	2.2
Persons	5.6	10.4	9.3	47.8	8.2	81.3	68.4	3.1	6.4	3.4
All modes										
Males	133.6	2.3	142.0	74.3	20.0	372.1	307.3	17.5	32.7	14.6
Females	94.9	27.0	48.5	96.2	41.8	308.4	255.2	14.9	24.7	13.6
Persons	228.5	29.3	190.5	170.5	61.7	680.5	562.5	32.4	57.4	28.2
STUDENTS AGED 19 AND OVER										
Full-time and sandwich										
Males	21.9	0.4	5.8	8.5	6.4	42.9	32.8	1.6	7.4	1.1
Females	20.9	4.3	7.1	10.1	12.2	54.6	41.2	2.3	9.5	1.6
Persons	42.8	4.7	12.9	18.6	18.5	97.5	74.0	4.0	16.9	2.7
Part-time day										
Males	44.5	3.9	68.9	13.1	21.1	151.4	128.5	6.5	12.9	3.5
Females	24.7	27.9	41.5	27.4	36.0	157.5	136.2	5.0	12.9	3.4
Persons	69.2	31.8	110.4	40.5	57.1	308.9	264.7	11.5	25.9	6.9
Evening only										
Males	15.6	8.9	53.4	55.5	30.7	164.1	142.2	5.9	12.1	3.9
Females	17.4	63.8	27.5	104.2	37.2	250.2	208.6	11.0	21.9	8.8
Persons	33.0	72.7	80.9	159.7	67.9	414.3	350.8	16.9	34.0	12.7
All modes										
Males	82.0	13.2	128.0	77.0	58.2	358.4	303.5	14.0	32.4	8.5
Females	63.1	96.0	76.2	141.7	85.4	462.3	385.9	18.3	44.3	13.8
Persons	145.1	109.2	204.2	218.8	143.5	820.7	689.4	32.3	76.7	22.3
STUDENTS ALL AGES										
Full-time and sandwich										
Males	94.7	0.9	28.4	55.2	15.9	195.0	161.6	10.0	16.4	7.0
Females	88.2	12.9	30.0	67.4	41.0	239.5	199.0	12.9	18.9	8.7
Persons	182.9	13.8	58.4	122.6	56.9	434.5	360.6	22.9	36.0 (4)	15.7
Part-time day										
Males	102.2	5.2	181.4	21.3	28.4	338.5	278.5	14.6	34.3	11.0
Females	49.9	36.4	64.7	37.8	43.9	232.7	193.6	7.3	24.1	7.7
Persons	152.2	41.6	246.1	59.1	72.2	571.2	472.2	21.9	60.7 (4)	18.7
Evening only										
Males	18.7	9.4	60.1	74.9	33.9	197.1	170.7	7.0	14.3	5.1
Females	19.9	73.7	30.1	132.7	42.2	298.6	248.5	13.0	26.1	11.0
Persons	38.6	83.1	90.2	207.6	76.2	495.6	419.2	19.9	43.0 (4)	16.1
All modes										
Males	215.6	15.5	270.0	151.3	78.1	730.5	610.8	31.6	65.1	23.1
Females	158.0	122.9	124.7	237.9	127.1	770.7	641.2	33.1	69.1	27.3
Persons	373.6	138.4	394.7	389.3	205.2	1,501.2	1,251.9	64.7	139.8 (4)	50.4
ALL MODES 1989										
Males	214.3	14.3	281.5	156.1	79.5	745.7	617.2	30.5	74.9	23.1
Females	151.5	120.3	124.5	241.1	119.2	756.6	623.4	30.6	75.2	27.3
Persons	365.8	134.6	406.0	397.2	198.6	1,502.3	1,240.6	61.1	150.1	50.4
ALL MODES 1985										
Males	181.0	7.7	232.2	157.4	56.6	634.9	521.5	25.5	70.7	17.2
Females	107.2	82.3	93.2	223.0	83.1	588.8	479.1	22.6	66.4	20.7
Persons	288.2	90.0	325.4	380.3	139.7	1,223.7	1,000.6	48.0	137.1	37.9
ALL MODES 1979										
Males	156.7	..	341.1	130.4	61.2	689.5	570.9	30.9	68.0	19.7
Females	57.0	..	72.8	171.5	85.1	385.5	307.3	16.6	45.5	17.2
Persons	213.7	..	413.9	301.9	146.3	1,076.0	878.2	47.4	113.5	36.9
ALL MODES 1975										
Males	73.9	..	419.0	163.3	69.7	725.9	} 621.2 {		87.4	17.3
Females	25.1	..	69.9	195.1	89.1	379.2	} 293.7 {		70.6	14.9
Persons	99.0	..	488.8	358.5	158.8	1,105.2	} 914.9 {		158.1	32.2

(1) Including BTEC first and national certificates and diplomas.
(2) SCOTVEC has superseded Royal Society of Arts and City and Guilds examinations in Scotland.
(3) Data for Northern Ireland relates to December 1989.
(4) Includes age and sex unknown for Scotland.

TABLE 25[27]: Students enrolled in Higher Education by type of establishment, sex, mode of attendance and level of course

(i) First year students (Home and Overseas)

Thousands

| | Universities(1)(2) | | | | | | | Other higher education(3)(4) | | | | | | |
| | Full-time | | | Part-time | | | Open Univer-sity(5) | Full-time | | | Part-time | | | All students |
	Under-graduate level	Post graduate level	Total	Under-graduate level	Post graduate level	Total		Under-graduate level	Post graduate level	Total	Under-graduate level	Post graduate level	Total	
1970/71														
Males	44	18	62	..	..	..	14	..	..	46	..	..	66	189
Females	21	7	28	..	..	..	5	..	..	45	..	..	7	85
Persons	66	25	90	..	..	..	20	..	..	91	..	..	73	274 (6)
1975/76														
Males	49	22	71	1	5	6	7	..	..	58	..	..	72	214
Females	27	9	37	1	2	3	5	..	..	48	..	..	14	107
Persons	77	31	108	2	7	9	12	..	..	106	..	..	87	322
1980/81(7)														
Males	52	20	72	1	6	7	8	52	6	58	80	5	85	230
Females	34	11	45	1	3	4	7	39	6	45	28	2	30	131
Persons	86	31	116	2	8	11	14	91	12	103	108	7	115	361 (8)
1985/86														
Males	49	24	73	2	8	10	14	63	6	68	87	6	93	258
Females	35	12	48	2	5	7	12	53	6	59	45	3	48	174
Persons	84	37	121	5	13	17	26	116	12	127	131	9	141	433 (8)
1989/90														
Males	56	25	81	2	10	12	16	71	7	78	90	8	98	285
Females	46	16	62	3	8	11	16	69	8	77	61	5	67	232
Persons	102	42	143	5	18	23	31	139	14	154	152	13	165	517 (8)
1990/91														
Males	58	27	85	2	11	14	17	80	8	89	90	9	100	304
Females	49	18	67	3	9	12	18	77	8	85	65	7	73	254
Persons	107	45	152	6	20	26	34	158	16	174	156	17	173	560 (8)

(ii) All students (Home and Overseas)

	Universities(1)(2) Full-time			Part-time			Open Univ.	Other higher ed. Full-time			Part-time			All students
1970/71														
Males	134	33	167	3	15	18	14	..	..	143	..	..	110	416
Females	59	10	68	2	3	6	5	..	..	30	..	..	12	205
Persons	192	43	235	5	18	23	20	..	..	172	..	..	121	621
1975/76														
Males	141	37	178	2	17	19	34	..	..	123	..	..	115	470
Females	77	13	91	2	5	7	22	..	..	123	..	..	21	264
Persons	218	51	269	4	23	26	56	..	..	246	..	..	137	734
1980/81(7)														
Males	157	34	191	2	20	23	38	120	7	127	135	11	146	524
Females	101	15	116	2	8	11	30	95	6	101	42	3	45	303
Persons	258	48	307	5	29	33	68	215	13	228	177	14	191	827 (8)
1985/86														
Males	148	37	185	5	22	26	42	146	7	154	134	12	146	553
Females	108	17	125	5	11	16	36	129	7	136	65	5	70	384
Persons	256	54	310	9	33	42	78	275	14	289	199	17	216	937 (8)
1989/90														
Males	161	39	200	5	26	31	47	161	8	169	143	16	159	605
Females	129	22	151	6	17	23	42	160	9	169	93	10	103	489
Persons	290	61	351	11	43	54	89	321	18	338	237	25	262	1,094 (8)
1990/91														
Males	167	41	208	5	27	32	49	180	10	190	143	18	161	641
Females	138	24	162	7	19	26	46	178	9	187	99	13	112	533
Persons	305	65	370	12	47	59	95	359	19	378	243	32	274	1,176

(1) See paragraph 12.2(i) of the explanatory notes.

(2) From 1971/72 onwards "undergraduate" includes first diplomas and certificates.

(3) Including certain students on courses not leading to a specified qualification; namely in Scotland new entrant students and from 1977/78 total students, in Northern Ireland total students in 1975/76. Includes grant-aided in Scotland.

(4) Excluding students in university departments of education, included under "Universities".

(5) Including associate and postgraduate students.

(6) Excluding a small number of part-time first year students in the universities.

(7) Split between undergraduate and postgraduate for Other higher education is estimated.

(8) In addition there were the following numbers of students in the United Kingdom enrolled on nursing and paramedical courses at Department of Health establishments :-

Thousands

| | Entrants | | | | All students | | | | |
	1980/81	1985/86	1989/90	1990/91	1980/81 *	1985/86	1989/90	1990/91	
Basic nursing courses	46	39	29	33	91	86	74	71	
Paramedical courses	3	3	4	4	10	9	10	11	
All courses	49	42	33	37	101	95	84	82	* Estimated

TABLE 26[28]: Students(1) enrolled in further and higher education by type of course, mode of study(2), sex and subject group(3), 1990/91(4)

(i) Home Students   Thousands

	Postgraduate level		First degree		Other higher education(5)		Total higher education		Further education(6)		ALL STUDENTS	
	Full-time	Part-time(7)	Full-time	Part-time(7)	Full-time	Part-time(7)	Full-time	Part-time(7)	Full-time	Part-time	Full-time	Part-time
PERSONS(8)												
Subject group												
1 Medicine & Dentistry	1.3	3.4	22.0	0.1	0.1	0.1	23.4	3.6	0.4	3.6	23.8	7.3
2 Allied Medicine	1.8	3.0	14.8	3.4	7.2	8.4	23.8	14.8	24.0	20.2	47.8	35.0
3 Biological Sciences	3.9	2.9	24.2	1.4	1.4	1.3	29.4	5.6	0.1	0.9	29.5	6.5
4 Agriculture	0.6	0.5	5.7	-	2.2	0.4	8.5	0.9	7.7	31.8	16.3	32.7
5 Physical Sciences	5.9	2.2	31.0	1.8	1.7	3.8	38.6	7.8	0.3	2.1	38.9	9.9
6 Mathematical Science	4.1	2.6	32.1	1.8	9.8	9.8	46.0	14.2	13.1	54.3	59.2	68.6
7 Engineering & Tech.	4.4	5.4	52.8	4.9	13.4	41.0	70.7	51.3	33.8	203.8	104.5	255.1
8 Architecture	1.9	3.1	15.7	4.2	4.0	20.9	21.6	28.2	18.9	117.2	40.5	145.3
9 Social Sciences	5.6	7.8	64.6	6.2	8.2	9.3	78.4	23.3	10.0	54.1	88.4	77.5
10 Business & Financial	4.2	21.5	46.7	6.7	31.7	92.0	82.6	120.3	104.3	311.6	186.9	431.9
11 Documentation	1.0	1.0	4.6	0.3	1.0	1.0	6.5	2.2	1.2	5.1	7.7	7.4
12 Languages	2.4	2.7	41.4	1.3	0.4	3.4	44.2	7.3	2.3	115.6	46.5	122.9
13 Humanities	1.9	3.2	22.3	1.2	0.1	0.6	24.4	5.0	0.1	2.7	24.5	7.7
14 Creative arts	2.8	1.4	33.4	0.9	12.5	1.4	48.6	3.7	59.0	127.8	107.6	131.5
15 Education(9)	11.7	14.9	24.0	3.6	3.1	10.9	38.7	29.4	5.3	60.0	44.0	89.4
16 Combined, gen	1.3	2.6	79.1	7.3	2.4	3.9	82.8	13.8	42.8	320.7	125.6	334.6
17 GCSE, SCE and CSE	-	-	-	-	-	-	-	-	120.8	257.8	120.8	257.8
ALL SUBJECTS(10)	54.8	78.0	514.5	45.1	99.1	208.3	668.4	331.4	473.0	1,751.2	1,141.4	2,082.6
MALES												
Subject group												
1 Medicine & Dentistry	0.6	1.9	11.6	0.1	0.1	0.1	12.3	2.0	0.2	0.4	12.4	2.5
2 Allied Medicine	0.7	1.1	4.0	0.7	1.0	1.9	5.6	3.7	1.0	4.0	6.7	7.7
3 Biological Sciences	2.1	1.5	10.4	0.5	0.7	0.4	13.2	2.4	-	0.2	13.2	2.6
4 Agriculture	0.3	0.3	3.0	-	1.4	0.2	4.7	0.5	4.6	16.4	9.3	17.0
5 Physical Sciences	4.6	1.7	21.0	1.2	1.2	2.2	26.8	5.1	0.2	1.6	26.9	6.7
6 Mathematical Science	3.1	1.9	23.7	1.5	7.2	6.3	34.0	9.7	9.7	24.6	43.7	34.3
7 Engineering & Tech.	3.8	4.9	45.8	4.6	11.3	38.7	61.0	48.2	30.5	186.2	91.4	234.4
8 Architecture	1.3	2.0	12.2	3.6	3.5	18.6	17.0	24.3	18.0	111.4	34.9	135.7
9 Social Sciences	2.6	4.0	30.9	2.9	2.8	2.7	36.3	9.6	1.9	11.5	38.1	21.1
10 Business & Financial	2.5	15.0	24.1	3.7	14.5	45.2	41.0	63.9	36.3	77.8	77.3	141.8
11 Documentation	0.4	0.4	1.4	0.1	0.5	0.2	2.3	0.6	0.6	2.4	2.9	3.0
12 Languages	1.1	1.1	11.4	0.4	0.1	1.0	12.6	2.5	0.7	47.0	13.4	49.5
13 Humanities	1.2	1.9	10.6	0.5	0.1	0.2	11.9	2.7	-	0.8	11.9	3.5
14 Creative arts	1.4	0.7	13.1	0.3	6.0	0.5	20.5	1.5	20.4	28.0	40.9	29.5
15 Education(9)	3.8	6.0	4.6	0.9	0.8	3.3	9.2	10.3	2.8	21.0	12.1	31.3
16 Combined, gen	0.6	1.1	35.1	2.7	1.1	1.5	36.8	5.3	20.4	105.5	57.2	110.8
17 GCSE, SCE and CSE	-	-	-	-	-	-	-	-	54.1	93.2	54.1	93.2
ALL SUBJECTS(10)	30.0	45.3	262.9	23.7	52.1	123.3	345.0	192.3	214.8	765.2	559.8	957.6
FEMALES												
Subject group												
1 Medicine & Dentistry	0.7	1.5	10.4	0.1	-	-	11.2	1.6	0.2	3.2	11.4	4.8
2 Allied Medicine	1.1	1.9	10.8	2.7	6.2	6.5	18.2	11.1	23.0	16.0	41.2	27.1
3 Biological Sciences	1.8	1.4	13.7	0.9	0.7	0.8	16.3	3.2	-	0.4	16.3	3.6
4 Agriculture	0.3	0.2	2.7	-	0.8	0.2	3.8	0.4	2.8	15.0	6.7	15.3
5 Physical Sciences	1.3	0.5	10.0	0.6	0.5	1.6	11.8	2.7	0.1	0.5	11.9	3.2
6 Mathematical Science	1.0	0.7	8.4	0.3	2.5	3.5	11.9	4.5	3.4	29.3	15.3	33.8
7 Engineering & Tech.	0.6	0.5	6.9	0.3	1.7	2.0	9.3	2.8	3.3	17.4	12.6	20.1
8 Architecture	0.6	1.0	3.6	0.6	0.5	2.2	4.7	3.8	0.9	5.6	5.5	9.4
9 Social Sciences	3.0	3.9	33.8	3.3	5.4	6.6	42.1	13.7	8.2	42.4	50.3	56.1
10 Business & Financial	1.8	6.5	22.6	3.0	16.9	46.3	41.2	55.8	67.7	232.7	108.9	288.4
11 Documentation	0.6	0.6	3.2	0.2	0.5	0.7	4.2	1.6	0.5	2.8	4.8	4.3
12 Languages	1.3	1.5	30.0	0.9	0.3	2.4	31.6	4.8	1.6	67.6	33.2	72.4
13 Humanities	0.7	1.3	11.7	0.7	-	0.4	12.5	2.3	-	1.7	12.5	4.0
14 Creative arts	1.4	0.7	20.3	0.6	6.4	0.9	28.1	2.2	38.6	99.8	66.7	101.9
15 Education(9)	7.9	8.9	19.4	2.7	2.2	7.6	29.4	19.1	2.5	39.0	31.9	58.1
16 Combined, gen	0.7	1.5	44.0	4.6	1.3	2.4	46.0	8.5	22.3	214.9	68.4	223.4
17 GCSE, SCE and CSE	-	-	-	-	-	-	-	-	66.6	164.6	66.6	164.6
ALL SUBJECTS(10)	24.8	32.7	251.4	21.4	46.1	83.9	322.3	137.9	257.4	981.1	579.8	1,119.0

(1) Excluding 81,700 (provisional) students on nursing and paramedical courses at Department of Health establishments.

(2) Full-time includes sandwich, part-time comprises both day and evening.

(3) Excluding data for school pupils, and for the Open University for which subject detail in this format is not available. The subject groups have been revised from the 12 groups previously used (up to 1987/88) and therefore individual subjects cannot be compared to earlier years.

(4) Data for Northern Ireland relates to 1989/90.

(5) Including courses regarded as equivalent to a first degree.

(6) Including 647,000 students in all modes in England, Wales and Northern Ireland who are taking unspecified courses.

(7) For Universities, part-time overseas students are recorded in this table as home students.

(8) Scotland figures include sex unknown.

(9) Includes Teacher Training enrolments for Universities only. Others included under the subject of study.

(10) Further Education totals include students in Scotland who are taking National Certificate Modules (90,600 Persons).

TABLE 26[28]: Students(1) enrolled in further and higher education by type of course, mode of study(2), sex and subject group(3), 1990/91(4)

(ii) Overseas Students   Thousands

	Postgraduate level		First degree		Other higher education(5)		Total higher education		Further education(6)		ALL STUDENTS	
	Full-time	Part-time(7)	Full-time	Part-time(7)	Full-time	Part-time(7)	Full-time	Part-time(7)	Full-time	Part-time	Full-time	Part-time
PERSONS(8)												
Subject group												
1 Medicine & Dentistry	1.3	-	1.6	-	0.1	-	3.0	-	-	-	3.0	-
2 Allied Medicine	0.6	-	1.1	-	0.2	0.1	2.0	0.1	0.1	-	2.1	0.1
3 Biological Sciences	1.5	-	1.2	-	0.2	-	2.9	-	-	-	2.9	-
4 Agriculture	1.0	-	0.4	-	0.2	-	1.6	-	0.2	0.1	1.8	0.1
5 Physical Sciences	2.0	-	1.1	-	0.2	-	3.3	-	-	-	3.3	-
6 Mathematical Science	1.8	-	2.3	-	0.4	-	4.5	0.1	0.2	0.2	4.6	0.2
7 Engineering & Tech.	5.2	0.2	8.8	-	1.4	0.1	15.5	0.3	0.9	0.3	16.4	0.7
8 Architecture	0.8	-	1.6	-	0.3	-	2.7	0.1	0.1	0.1	2.8	0.2
9 Social Sciences	5.3	-	6.2	-	0.9	-	12.5	-	0.1	-	12.6	0.1
10 Business & Financial	3.6	0.3	5.6	-	2.2	0.2	11.4	0.5	1.3	0.8	12.7	1.3
11 Documentation	0.4	-	0.2	-	-	-	0.6	-	-	-	0.7	-
12 Languages	1.7	-	1.8	-	1.0	0.2	4.5	0.2	1.6	3.9	6.1	4.1
13 Humanities	1.3	-	0.6	-	0.2	-	2.2	-	-	-	2.2	-
14 Creative arts	0.6	-	1.4	-	0.5	-	2.5	-	0.7	0.1	3.2	0.2
15 Education(9)	1.6	-	0.5	-	0.2	-	2.3	-	-	0.1	2.3	0.1
16 Combined, gen	0.3	-	4.3	-	4.1	0.1	8.8	0.2	0.5	1.0	9.3	1.2
17 GCSE, SCE and CSE	-	-	-	-	-	-	-	-	1.5	0.5	1.5	0.5
ALL SUBJECTS(10)	29.1	0.7	38.7	0.2	12.4	0.7	80.2	1.6	7.5	7.3	87.7	8.9
MALES												
Subject group												
1 Medicine & Dentistry	0.9	-	1.0	-	0.1	-	1.9	-	-	-	2.0	-
2 Allied Medicine	0.4	-	0.4	-	0.1	-	0.8	-	-	-	0.9	-
3 Biological Sciences	0.9	-	0.4	-	0.1	-	1.4	-	-	-	1.4	-
4 Agriculture	0.8	-	0.2	-	0.1	-	1.1	-	0.1	-	1.2	-
5 Physical Sciences	1.6	-	0.7	-	0.1	-	2.4	-	-	-	2.4	-
6 Mathematical Science	1.4	-	1.5	-	0.3	-	3.2	0.1	0.1	0.1	3.3	0.1
7 Engineering & Tech.	4.7	0.2	7.9	-	1.3	0.1	14.0	0.3	0.9	0.3	14.8	0.6
8 Architecture	0.6	-	1.1	-	0.2	-	1.9	0.1	0.1	0.1	2.0	0.1
9 Social Sciences	3.5	-	3.2	-	0.5	-	7.2	-	-	-	7.2	-
10 Business & Financial	2.5	0.2	3.0	-	1.2	0.1	6.7	0.4	0.5	0.3	7.3	0.7
11 Documentation	0.2	-	0.1	-	-	-	0.3	-	-	-	0.3	-
12 Languages	0.8	-	0.5	-	0.3	0.1	1.5	0.1	0.7	0.9	2.2	1.0
13 Humanities	0.8	-	0.3	-	0.1	-	1.1	-	-	-	1.1	-
14 Creative arts	0.3	-	0.5	-	0.2	-	1.0	-	0.2	-	1.2	-
15 Education(9)	0.8	-	0.2	-	0.1	-	1.1	-	-	-	1.1	-
16 Combined, gen	0.2	-	2.1	-	1.7	-	4.1	0.1	0.2	0.3	4.3	0.4
17 GCSE, SCE and CSE	-	-	-	-	-	-	-	-	0.9	0.2	0.9	0.2
ALL SUBJECTS(10)	20.2	0.5	23.2	0.1	6.4	0.5	49.7	1.1	4.0	2.3	53.7	3.4
FEMALES												
Subject group												
1 Medicine & Dentistry	0.4	-	0.6	-	-	-	1.1	-	-	-	1.1	-
2 Allied Medicine	0.3	-	0.7	-	0.2	-	1.2	-	-	-	1.2	0.1
3 Biological Sciences	0.6	-	0.7	-	0.1	-	1.5	-	-	-	1.5	-
4 Agriculture	0.2	-	0.2	-	-	-	0.5	-	-	-	0.5	-
5 Physical Sciences	0.4	-	0.4	-	0.1	-	0.9	-	-	-	0.9	-
6 Mathematical Science	0.4	-	0.7	-	0.2	-	1.3	-	0.1	0.1	1.4	0.1
7 Engineering & Tech.	0.5	-	0.9	-	0.1	-	1.5	-	0.1	-	1.6	-
8 Architecture	0.2	-	0.5	-	0.1	-	0.8	-	-	-	0.8	-
9 Social Sciences	1.8	-	3.0	-	0.5	-	5.3	-	0.1	-	5.4	0.1
10 Business & Financial	1.1	-	2.6	-	0.9	-	4.6	0.1	0.8	0.5	5.4	0.6
11 Documentation	0.2	-	0.1	-	-	-	0.4	-	-	-	0.4	-
12 Languages	0.9	-	1.3	-	0.7	0.1	3.0	0.1	0.9	3.0	3.9	3.1
13 Humanities	0.5	-	0.4	-	0.1	-	1.0	-	-	-	1.0	-
14 Creative arts	0.3	-	0.9	-	0.3	-	1.5	-	0.5	0.1	2.0	0.1
15 Education(9)	0.8	-	0.3	-	0.1	-	1.2	-	-	-	1.2	0.1
16 Combined, gen	0.1	-	2.2	-	2.4	0.1	4.8	0.1	0.3	0.7	5.1	0.8
17 GCSE, SCE and CSE	-	-	-	-	-	-	-	-	0.6	0.3	0.6	0.3
ALL SUBJECTS(10)	8.9	0.1	15.5	0.1	6.0	0.3	30.5	0.5	3.5	5.0	34.0	5.5

For footnotes see Table 26 (i).

FURTHER AND HIGHER EDUCATION

TABLE 26[28]: Students(1) enrolled in further and higher education by type of course, mode of study(2), sex and subject group(3), 1990/91(4)

(iii) Home and Overseas Students — Thousands

Subject group	Postgraduate level Full-time	Part-time	First degree Full-time	Part-time	Other higher education(5) Full-time	Part-time	Total higher education Full-time	Part-time	Further education(6) Full-time	Part-time	ALL STUDENTS Full-time	Part-time
PERSONS(8)												
Subject group												
1 Medicine & Dentistry	2.6	3.4	23.6	0.1	0.2	0.1	26.4	3.6	0.4	3.6	26.8	7.3
2 Allied Medicine	2.4	3.0	15.9	3.4	7.4	8.5	25.8	14.8	24.1	20.3	49.9	35.1
3 Biological Sciences	5.4	2.9	25.3	1.4	1.6	1.3	32.3	5.6	0.1	1.0	32.4	6.5
4 Agriculture	1.7	0.5	6.1	-	2.3	0.4	10.1	0.9	7.9	31.9	18.0	32.8
5 Physical Sciences	7.9	2.2	32.1	1.8	1.9	3.8	41.9	7.8	0.3	2.1	42.2	10.0
6 Mathematical Science	5.9	2.6	34.4	1.8	10.3	9.9	50.5	14.3	13.3	54.5	63.8	68.8
7 Engineering & Tech.	9.7	5.6	61.6	4.9	14.8	41.2	86.1	51.7	34.8	204.1	120.9	255.8
8 Architecture	2.6	3.1	17.4	4.3	4.3	20.9	24.3	28.3	19.0	117.2	43.3	145.5
9 Social Sciences	11.0	7.9	70.9	6.2	9.1	9.3	90.9	23.4	10.1	54.2	101.0	77.5
10 Business & Financial	7.8	21.8	52.3	6.7	33.9	92.2	94.0	120.7	105.6	312.4	199.6	433.2
11 Documentation	1.4	1.0	4.8	0.3	1.0	1.0	7.2	2.2	1.2	5.2	8.4	7.4
12 Languages	4.2	2.7	43.2	1.3	1.4	3.5	48.8	7.5	3.9	119.6	52.7	127.0
13 Humanities	3.2	3.2	23.0	1.2	0.4	0.6	26.5	5.0	0.1	2.7	26.6	7.7
14 Creative arts	3.4	1.4	34.7	0.9	13.0	1.4	51.1	3.7	59.7	127.9	110.8	131.7
15 Education(9)	13.3	14.9	24.5	3.6	3.3	10.9	41.0	29.4	5.3	60.1	46.3	89.5
16 Combined, gen	1.6	2.6	83.4	7.3	6.6	4.1	91.6	14.0	43.3	321.8	135.0	335.8
17 GCSE, SCE and CSE	-	-	-	-	-	-	-	-	122.4	258.4	122.4	258.4
ALL SUBJECTS(10)	83.9	78.6	553.2	45.2	111.5	209.1	748.6	332.9	480.4	1,758.5	1,229.0	2,091.5
MALES												
Subject group												
1 Medicine & Dentistry	1.5	1.9	12.6	0.1	0.1	0.1	14.2	2.0	0.2	0.4	14.4	2.5
2 Allied Medicine	1.0	1.1	4.4	0.7	1.1	2.0	6.5	3.7	1.0	4.0	7.5	7.7
3 Biological Sciences	3.0	1.5	10.9	0.5	0.7	0.4	14.6	2.4	-	0.2	14.6	2.6
4 Agriculture	1.2	0.3	3.2	-	1.5	0.2	5.8	0.5	4.8	16.5	10.6	17.0
5 Physical Sciences	6.1	1.7	21.7	1.2	1.3	2.2	29.2	5.1	0.2	1.6	29.3	6.7
6 Mathematical Science	4.5	1.9	25.3	1.5	7.5	6.3	37.2	9.8	9.8	24.7	47.0	34.4
7 Engineering & Tech.	8.5	5.0	53.8	4.7	12.6	38.8	74.9	48.5	31.3	186.5	106.2	235.0
8 Architecture	1.8	2.1	13.3	3.6	3.7	18.6	18.8	24.3	18.1	111.5	36.9	135.8
9 Social Sciences	6.1	4.0	34.1	2.9	3.2	2.7	43.5	9.6	1.9	11.5	45.4	21.2
10 Business & Financial	4.9	15.2	27.1	3.8	15.7	45.3	47.8	64.3	36.8	78.2	84.6	142.5
11 Documentation	0.6	0.4	1.5	0.1	0.5	0.2	2.6	0.6	0.6	2.4	3.2	3.0
12 Languages	1.9	1.1	11.9	0.4	0.4	1.1	14.1	2.6	1.4	47.9	15.6	50.5
13 Humanities	2.0	1.9	10.9	0.5	0.2	0.2	13.0	2.7	-	0.8	13.1	3.5
14 Creative arts	1.6	0.7	13.6	0.3	6.2	0.5	21.5	1.5	20.6	28.0	42.1	29.5
15 Education(9)	4.6	6.0	4.8	0.9	0.9	3.3	10.3	10.3	2.8	21.0	13.2	31.3
16 Combined, gen	0.8	1.1	37.2	2.7	2.8	1.6	40.8	5.4	20.6	105.8	61.5	111.2
17 GCSE, SCE and CSE	-	-	-	-	-	-	-	-	55.1	93.4	55.1	93.4
ALL SUBJECTS(10)	50.1	45.9	286.1	23.8	58.5	123.8	394.7	193.4	218.8	767.5	613.5	961.0
FEMALES												
Subject group												
1 Medicine & Dentistry	1.1	1.5	11.0	0.1	0.1	-	12.2	1.6	0.2	3.2	12.4	4.8
2 Allied Medicine	1.4	1.9	11.6	2.7	6.4	6.5	19.3	11.1	23.0	16.0	42.4	27.1
3 Biological Sciences	2.4	1.4	14.5	0.9	0.8	0.8	17.8	3.2	-	0.4	17.8	3.6
4 Agriculture	0.5	0.2	2.9	-	0.9	0.2	4.3	0.4	2.9	15.0	7.2	15.4
5 Physical Sciences	1.7	0.5	10.4	0.6	0.6	1.6	12.7	2.7	0.1	0.5	12.8	3.2
6 Mathematical Science	1.4	0.7	9.1	0.3	2.7	3.5	13.2	4.5	3.5	29.4	16.7	33.9
7 Engineering & Tech.	1.2	0.6	7.8	0.3	1.8	2.0	10.8	2.8	3.4	17.4	14.2	20.2
8 Architecture	0.8	1.0	4.1	0.6	0.6	2.2	5.5	3.8	0.9	5.6	6.4	9.5
9 Social Sciences	4.8	3.9	36.7	3.3	5.9	6.6	47.4	13.7	8.2	42.4	55.7	56.2
10 Business & Financial	2.9	6.6	25.2	3.0	17.8	46.3	45.8	55.9	68.5	233.1	114.3	289.0
11 Documentation	0.8	0.6	3.3	0.2	0.6	0.7	4.6	1.6	0.5	2.8	5.2	4.4
12 Languages	2.3	1.5	31.3	0.9	1.0	2.4	34.6	4.9	2.5	70.6	37.1	75.5
13 Humanities	1.3	1.3	12.0	0.7	0.2	0.4	13.5	2.3	-	1.7	13.5	4.0
14 Creative arts	1.7	0.7	21.1	0.6	6.7	0.9	29.6	2.2	39.1	99.9	68.7	102.1
15 Education(9)	8.6	8.9	19.7	2.7	2.3	7.6	30.6	19.1	2.5	39.1	33.1	58.2
16 Combined, gen	0.8	1.5	46.2	4.7	3.8	2.5	50.8	8.6	22.6	215.7	73.4	224.3
17 GCSE, SCE and CSE	-	-	-	-	-	-	-	-	67.3	164.9	67.3	164.9
ALL SUBJECTS(10)	33.8	32.8	266.9	21.4	52.1	84.2	352.8	138.4	260.9	986.1	613.7	1,124.5

For footnotes see Table 26 (i).

TABLE 27[29]: Countries of domicile and study of full-time and sandwich students enrolled in higher education, 1990/91

Thousands

	COUNTRY OF STUDY									
	Postgraduates					First degree and other higher education				
	England	Wales	Scotland	N Ireland	UK	England	Wales	Scotland	N Ireland	UK
COUNTRY OF DOMICILE										
Home students										
Universities	30.2	2.4	4.5	1.5	38.6	198.8	18.3	41.9	13.9	273.0
Polytechnics and other H/E(1)	13.0	0.4	2.7	0.1	16.2	285.3	13.4	38.6	3.3	340.7
Total	43.2	2.8	7.2	1.6	54.8	484.2	31.7	80.5	17.2	613.6
Students from overseas(2)										
Universities	21.9	1.4	3.1	0.3	26.7	23.9	1.6	4.5	2.0	32.0
Polytechnics and other H/E(1)	2.1	0.1	0.2	-	2.4	17.4	0.7	0.8	0.1	19.1
Total	24.0	1.5	3.3	0.3	29.1	41.4	2.3	5.3	2.1	51.1
Grand total all students	67.2	4.3	10.5	1.9	83.9	525.6	34.0	85.8	19.3	664.7
Country of domicile of home students										
England	40.3	1.3	1.6	0.1	43.1	454.9	18.1	11.3	0.6	484.9
Wales	1.4	1.5	0.1	-	2.9	18.2	13.0	0.3	-	31.5
Scotland	1.1	-	5.2	-	6.4	4.6	0.2	64.5	0.1	69.4
Northern Ireland	0.5	-	0.2	1.5	2.2	6.5	0.3	2.1	16.5	25.5
UK not known	-	-	0.2	-	0.2	-	-	2.3	-	2.3
Domicile of students from overseas										
European Community	5.4	0.3	0.7	0.1	6.5	13.6	0.7	1.8	1.7	17.8
Other Europe	1.1	-	0.2	-	1.3	3.1	0.1	0.8	-	4.1
Commonwealth	8.0	0.6	1.1	0.1	9.8	19.2	1.2	1.6	0.3	22.4
Other Countries	9.5	0.6	1.4	0.1	11.6	5.7	0.2	1.1	0.1	7.1
All students from overseas	24.0	1.5	3.3	0.3	29.1	41.6	2.3	5.3	2.1	51.3

	All higher education				
	England	Wales	Scotland	N Ireland	UK
COUNTRY OF DOMICILE					
Home students					
Universities	229.0	20.7	46.4	15.4	311.5
Polytechnics and other H/E(1)	298.4	13.8	41.3	3.4	356.9
Total	527.4	34.5	87.7	18.8	668.4
Students from overseas(2)					
Universities	45.8	3.0	7.6	2.3	58.7
Polytechnics and other H/E(1)	19.6	0.8	1.0	0.1	21.5
Total	65.4	3.8	8.6	2.4	80.2
Grand total all students	592.8	38.3	96.3	21.2	748.6
Country of domicile of home students					
England	495.1	19.4	12.8	0.6	528.0
Wales	19.5	14.5	0.4	-	34.4
Scotland	5.7	0.2	69.7	0.1	75.8
Northern Ireland	7.0	0.3	2.3	18.0	27.6
UK not known	-	-	2.5	-	2.6
Domicile of students from overseas					
European Community	19.0	1.0	2.4	1.8	24.3
Other Europe	4.2	0.1	1.0	-	5.4
Commonwealth	27.3	1.8	2.7	0.4	32.2
Other Countries	15.2	0.8	2.5	0.1	18.7
All students from overseas	65.6	3.8	8.6	2.4	80.5

(1) Including grant-aided in Scotland.

(2) See paragraph 12.11 of the explanatory notes.

TABLE 28 [30]:   Full-time students from overseas, 1990/91

(i) Enrolments by type of course, sex and country, in higher and further education

		Higher education			Further education	1990/91 Higher and Further Education			1989/90			Thousands 1980/81
		Post-graduate	First degree	Other		Males	Females	Persons	Males	Females	Persons	Persons
RANK	TOP FIFTY NAMED COUNTRIES											
1	Malaysia	1.3	6.0	0.3	0.3	4.7	3.2	7.9	4.5	3.0	7.5	13.3
2	Hong Kong	1.3	5.0	0.4	1.0	5.0	2.7	7.7	5.0	2.5	7.6	7.2
3	USA	1.5	0.8	3.1	0.1	2.5	3.0	5.5	2.5	3.2	5.7	2.9
4	Ireland. Republic of	0.6	3.4	0.7	0.5	2.6	2.7	5.2	2.2	2.3	4.5	0.5
5	West Germany	1.0	2.2	1.6	0.2	2.6	2.3	4.9	2.1	2.0	4.1	1.3
6	France	0.9	2.1	1.2	0.4	2.3	2.3	4.6	1.7	1.9	3.6	0.7
7	Greece	2.0	1.7	0.3	0.3	3.0	1.3	4.3	2.4	1.0	3.4	2.5
8	Singapore	0.5	1.9	0.1	-	1.6	0.9	2.5	1.4	0.8	2.2	1.6
9	Spain	0.6	0.9	0.4	0.4	1.1	1.1	2.3	1.0	0.9	1.9	..
10	Cyprus	0.3	1.4	0.2	0.1	1.2	0.7	1.9	1.1	0.6	1.7	1.5
11	Japan	0.7	0.4	0.3	0.4	0.7	1.1	1.8	0.6	0.9	1.5	..
12	Norway	0.3	1.4	0.1	-	1.1	0.7	1.8	1.0	0.6	1.7	0.5
13	China, People's Republic of	1.5	0.1	-	0.1	1.3	0.4	1.7	1.2	0.4	1.6	0.2
14	Italy	0.4	0.7	0.4	0.1	0.8	0.8	1.6	0.7	0.7	1.3	..
15	Kenya	0.5	0.8	0.1	0.1	0.9	0.5	1.4	0.9	0.4	1.3	1.1
16	Pakistan	0.8	0.3	0.1	0.1	1.1	0.2	1.3	1.1	0.1	1.3	0.8
17	India	0.7	0.2	0.1	0.1	0.9	0.3	1.2	0.9	0.3	1.1	0.9
18	Turkey	0.8	0.1	-	0.2	0.8	0.3	1.1	0.7	0.2	0.9	..
19	Canada	0.7	0.3	0.1	-	0.6	0.5	1.1	0.6	0.5	1.0	0.7
20	Netherlands	0.3	0.5	0.2	0.1	0.6	0.5	1.1	0.5	0.4	0.9	..
21	Nigeria	0.6	0.3	0.1	0.1	0.7	0.3	1.1	0.8	0.3	1.2	5.2
22	Brazil	0.9	-	-	-	0.6	0.4	0.9	0.5	0.3	0.8	0.5
23	Belgium	0.2	0.5	0.1	0.1	0.5	0.4	0.9	0.4	0.3	0.7	..
24	Israel	0.2	0.6	-	-	0.6	0.2	0.8	0.5	0.1	0.6	..
25	Brunei	0.1	0.5	0.2	-	0.5	0.3	0.8	0.5	0.3	0.9	1.0
26	Taiwan	0.4	0.1	-	0.2	0.4	0.4	0.7	0.2	0.2	0.4	..
27	Sri Lanka	0.2	0.4	0.1	0.1	0.5	0.2	0.7	0.5	0.2	0.7	1.2
28	South Africa	0.3	0.3	0.1	0.1	0.5	0.3	0.7	0.5	0.3	0.7	..
29	Zambia	0.2	0.3	0.1	0.1	0.5	0.2	0.7	0.5	0.1	0.7	0.8
30	Iran	0.4	0.2	-	0.1	0.5	0.1	0.7	0.7	0.2	0.9	6.6
31	Denmark	0.2	0.2	0.1	-	0.3	0.3	0.6	0.2	0.2	0.5	..
32	Oman	-	0.2	0.1	0.2	0.5	0.1	0.6	0.5	0.1	0.6	..
33	Saudi Arabia	0.4	0.1	-	0.1	0.5	0.1	0.6	0.5	0.1	0.6	0.4
34	South Korea	0.4	0.1	-	-	0.5	0.1	0.6	0.4	0.1	0.5	..
35	Australia	0.4	0.1	-	-	0.3	0.2	0.6	0.3	0.2	0.5	..
36	Portugal	0.2	0.2	-	0.1	0.3	0.2	0.5	0.3	0.2	0.5	..
37	Indonesia	0.4	0.1	-	-	0.4	0.1	0.5	0.5	0.1	0.6	..
38	Thailand	0.3	0.1	-	0.1	0.3	0.3	0.5	0.2	0.2	0.5	..
39	Zimbabwe	0.2	0.2	0.1	0.1	0.3	0.2	0.5	0.4	0.1	0.5	..
40	Tanzania	0.3	0.1	0.1	-	0.4	0.1	0.5	0.4	0.1	0.5	0.7
41	Mauritius	-	0.3	0.1	-	0.3	0.2	0.5	0.3	0.2	0.4	..
42	Botswana	0.1	0.2	0.1	-	0.3	0.1	0.4	0.3	0.1	0.4	..
43	Switzerland	0.1	0.2	-	-	0.2	0.2	0.4	0.2	0.2	0.4	..
44	Bangladesh	0.3	-	-	-	0.3	0.1	0.4	0.3	0.1	0.4	..
45	Jordan	0.2	0.2	-	-	0.3	0.1	0.4	0.4	0.1	0.5	1.2
46	Sudan	0.3	0.1	-	-	0.3	0.1	0.4	0.3	0.1	0.4	1.0
47	Malawi	0.1	0.2	0.1	-	0.3	0.1	0.4	0.4	0.1	0.5	..
48	Ghana	0.2	0.1	-	-	0.3	0.1	0.4	0.3	0.1	0.4	0.7
49	Mexico	0.3	-	-	-	0.3	0.1	0.4	0.2	0.1	0.3	..
50	Iraq	0.3	0.1	-	-	0.3	-	0.4	0.5	-	0.6	2.2
	Other/unknown	4.2	2.8	1.0	1.0	6.1	3.0	9.1	6.2	2.7	8.6	18.4
	TOTAL	29.1	38.7	12.4	7.3	53.6	33.9	87.6	50.3	30.1	80.5	75.6

TABLE 28 [30] (continued):   Full-time students from overseas, 1990/91

(ii) First Year Students and Enrolments by grouped country of domicile, in higher and further education(1)

MALES   Thousands

	First Year Students					All Enrolments				
	1975/76	1980/81 (2)	1985/86 (3)	1989/90	1990/91	1975/76 (4)	1980/81 (2)	1985/86 (3)	1989/90	1990/91
European Community	..	1.7	3.2	7.0	8.6 (5)	..	3.4	5.1	11.6	14.3 (5)
Other Europe	..	0.7	1.2	1.3	1.7	..	1.8	2.6	2.7	3.3
Commonwealth	..	13.4	12.0	10.9	11.3 (5)	..	29.5	21.6	21.9	22.7 (5)
Other Countries	..	10.1	10.3	8.8	8.2	..	21.8	15.8	14.2	13.5
All countries (6)	..	25.9	26.7	28.0	29.7 (5)		56.5	45.1	50.3	53.6 (5)
of which										
Higher education(6)	..	17.5	21.8	24.8	26.6	..	41.9	38.4	46.1	49.7
Further education	..	8.4	4.9	3.2	3.1	..	14.7	6.7	4.2	3.9

FEMALES

	First Year Students					All Enrolments				
	1975/76	1980/81 (2)	1985/86 (3)	1989/90	1990/91	1975/76 (4)	1980/81 (2)	1985/86 (3)	1989/90	1990/91
European Community	..	1.3	2.4	6.3	7.7 (5)	..	2.0	3.7	10.1	12.2 (5)
Other Europe	..	0.5	0.8	0.3	1.4	..	1.1	1.3	1.7	2.4
Commonwealth	..	4.8	4.9	5.5	6.0 (5)	..	10.1	8.6	11.1	12.1 (5)
Other Countries	..	3.1	3.8	6.2	5.3	..	5.7	5.0	7.3	7.3
All countries (6)	..	9.7	11.9	18.3	20.5 (5)		19.0	18.6	30.1	33.9 (5)
of which										
Higher education(6)	..	6.3	9.2	15.5	17.6	..	13.5	15.3	26.7	30.5
Further education	..	3.4	2.6	2.7	2.9	..	5.5	3.3	3.5	3.5

PERSONS

	First Year Students					All Enrolments				
	1975/76	1980/81 (2)	1985/86 (3)	1989/90	1990/91	1975/76 (4)	1980/81 (2)	1985/86 (3)	1989/90	1990/91
European Community	2.0	3.0	5.6	13.3	16.3 (5)	2.6	5.4	8.9	21.7	26.5 (5)
Other Europe	..	1.1	2.1	1.6	3.1	..	3.1	3.8	4.4	5.7
Commonwealth	23.6	18.1	16.9	16.4	17.3 (5)	39.8	39.6	30.2	32.9	34.7 (5)
Other Countries	21.1	13.4	13.9	14.9	13.5	34.1	27.4	20.8	21.4	20.8
All countries (6)	46.7	35.6	38.5	46.3	50.2 (5)	76.5	75.6	63.7	80.5	87.6 (5)
of which										
Higher education(6)	26.8	23.8	31.0	40.3	44.2	49.8	55.5	53.7	72.8	80.2
Further education	19.9	11.8	7.5	5.9	6.0	26.8	20.2	10.0	7.7	7.3

(1) Figures for Scotland are Autumn counts for vocational further education.

(2) Estimated.

(3) See paragraph 12.11 of explanatory notes for the change of definition of a "student from overseas".

(4) Great Britain only.

(5) Gibraltar is included in both EC and Commonwealth figures. Numbers in grouped countries do not sum to overall student numbers due to overlap.

(6) For 1985/86 and subsequent years, figures have been adjusted to take account of the change of definition of a "student from overseas".

QUALIFICATIONS AND DESTINATIONS

TABLE 29[31]: Pupils leaving school by sex and highest qualification held

(i) Time series   Thousands

	GREAT BRITAIN			UNITED KINGDOM				
	1980/81	1984/85	1985/86	1965/66	1975/76	1985/86	1989/90(1)	1990/91(1)
MALES								
Leavers with GCE A-levels/SCE H-grade passes								
2 or more A, 3 or more H	65	67	64	48	61	66	72	72
1 A, 1 or 2 H	15	15	15	12	15	16	16	14
Leavers with GCSE/GCE O-level/CSE/SCE O/standard grades alone								
5 or more A-C awards/CSE grade 1(2)	37	43	43	26	31	44	41	40
1-4 A-C awards/CSE grade 1(2)	109	108	106	54	101	108	93	85
No higher grades(3)								
5 or more other grades	89	90	85	}		86	52	55
1-4 other grades	60	61	63	} 234	216	65	53	42
No GCSE/GCE/SCE or CSE qualification	68	57	55	}		59	36	31
TOTAL SCHOOL LEAVERS	442	441	430	373	423	444	362	338
FEMALES								
Leavers with GCE A-levels/SCE H-grade passes								
2 or more A, 3 or more H	57	60	58	32	49	61	74	76
1 A, 1 or 2 H	17	19	18	11	16	18	17	17
Leavers with GCSE/GCE O-level/CSE/SCE O/standard grades alone								
5 or more A-C awards/CSE grade 1(2)	44	50	49	31	38	51	52	51
1-4 A-C awards/CSE grade 1(2)	120	124	119	56	108	123	97	87
No higher grades(3)								
5 or more other grades	81	80	79	}		80	42	41
1-4 other grades	54	51	51	} 222	190	52	37	30
No GCSE/GCE/SCE or CSE qualification	51	42	41	}		43	24	21
TOTAL SCHOOL LEAVERS	423	425	414	352	400	427	344	323

(ii) By country, 1990/91   Thousands

	UNITED KINGDOM	ENGLAND	WALES (1)	SCOTLAND	NORTHERN IRELAND
MALES					
Leavers with GCE A-levels/SCE H-grade passes					
2 or more A, 3 or more H	72	58	3	8	3
1 A, 1 or 2 H	14	10	1	4	-
Leavers with GCSE/GCE O-level/CSE/SCE O/standard grades alone					
5 or more A-C awards/CSE grade 1(2)	40	35	2	2	1
1-4 A-C awards/CSE grade 1(2)	85	71	4	8	3
No higher grades(3)					
5 or more other grades	55	52	}	2	1
1-4 other grades	42	29	} 5	6	1
No GCSE/GCE/SCE or CSE qualification	31	23	3	4	2
TOTAL SCHOOL LEAVERS	338	277	17	32	12
FEMALES					
Leavers with GCE A-levels/SCE H-grade passes					
2 or more A, 3 or more H	76	60	4	9	4
1 A, 1 or 2 H	17	11	1	5	-
Leavers with GCSE/GCE O-level/CSE/SCE O/standard grades alone					
5 or more A-C awards/CSE grade 1(2)	51	45	2	2	2
1-4 A-C awards/CSE grade 1(2)	87	73	4	7	3
No higher grades(3)					
5 or more other grades	41	39	}	1	1
1-4 other grades	30	21	} 4	4	1
No GCSE/GCE/SCE or CSE qualification	21	15	2	3	1
TOTAL SCHOOL LEAVERS	323	265	16	30	12

(1) No split available for 'No higher grades' for Wales. Figures are included in '1-4 other grades'.
(2) See paragraphs 13.2 to 13.4 of the explanatory notes.
(3) GCSE grades D-G, O-level grades D-E and CSE grades 2-5 in England and Wales.

TABLE 30[32]: GCSE/GCE/CSE qualifications and intended destination of pupils leaving school(1) during 1990/91

ENGLAND AND WALES   Thousands

| | Intended destination | | | | | | | | | All destinations | | |
| | Higher education(2) | | | Further education(2) | | | Available for employment(3) | | | | | |
	Males	Females	Persons	Males	Females	Persons	Males	Females	Persons	Males	Females	Persons
QUALIFICATIONS HELD ON LEAVING SCHOOL												
Leavers with A-level passes												
3 or more	36	34	70	2	2	4	8	8	17	46	45	91
2	8	10	18	2	2	4	5	6	11	15	18	34
1	4	3	6	2	3	4	5	6	11	11	12	22
Total	48	47	95	5	7	12	18	21	39	72	75	147
Leavers with GCSE/O-level/CSE alone												
5 or more A-C awards(4)/CSE grade 1	1	1	2	20	30	50	15	16	32	36	47	84
1-4 A-C awards(4)/CSE grade 1	1	1	2	27	35	62	46	41	87	74	77	151
Numbers with 2 or more A-level passes	44	44	89	4	4	8	13	15	28	61	63	124
Numbers with at least 5 A-C awards and/or at least 1 A-level pass	49	48	97	25	37	62	34	37	71	108	122	230

(1) Excluding those leaving from special schools.

(2) Previous versions of the table showed groupings for University and Further Education (including other higher education and teacher training).

(3) Including those leaving for temporary employment pending entry to full-time education and with destination not known.

(4) See paragraph 13.2 of the explanatory notes.

QUALIFICATIONS AND DESTINATIONS

TABLE 31[33]: Pupils leaving school with GCSE/GCE O-level/SCE grades (A-C)(1) and CSE grade 1 by subject and sex (2)

	ENGLAND AND WALES			GREAT BRITAIN			1990/91(3)			
	1970/71	1975/76	1980/81	1980/81	1985/86	1989/90(3)				PERSONS
			PERSONS				PERSONS	MALES	FEMALES	(000s)
Percentage obtaining GCSE/GCE O-level/ SCE (grades A-C) and CSE (grade 1) in										
English	34	36	37	38	41	49	51	44	58	324
History	14	14	15	15	15	17	18	16	20	112
French	15	14	14	15	15	20	22	17	27	140
Music, drama, visual arts	11	13	13	13	14	20	22	16	28	139
Mathematics	23	24	27	29	31	37	37	38	37	237
Physics	10	11	14	14	16	17	16	21	11	104
Chemistry	8	9	12	12	14	17	16	18	15	105
Biology	13	15	16	16	16	17	16	13	19	101
Other science(4)	10	11	11	11	12	18	20	25	14	125
Geography	15	16	16	16	17	19	20	22	19	129
Vocational subjects(5)	7	8	10	11	12	16	16	8	25	101
Any subject	43	50	53	53	55	64	65	61	70	417
English and mathematics	20	20	23	24	27	33	35	34	37	224
English, mathematics and science	16	16	19	19	22	28	30	30	29	188
English, mathematics, science and modern languages	10	10	11	11	12	17	19	16	22	123
ALL LEAVERS (thousands)	613	707	778	865	844	682	637	326	311	637

(1) See paragraph 13.2 of the explanatory notes.
(2) Irrespective of any A-levels/H grades obtained.
(3) Due to changes in subject classification, direct comparisons of individual subjects are not possible from 1989/90, with earlier years.
(4) Including metal work, woodwork and technical drawing.
(5) Including business and domestic subjects.

TABLE 32[34]: Pupils leaving school with 2 or more GCE A levels/3 or more SCE H grades (1) by subject combinations by subject and sex

	ENGLAND AND WALES			GREAT BRITAIN			1990/91(2)			
	1970/71	1975/76	1980/81	1980/81	1985/86	1989/90(2)				PERSONS
			PERSONS				PERSONS	MALES	FEMALES	(000s)
Percentage obtaining two or more A levels/three or more H grades										
Mathematics/science	23	20	22	20	22	11	10	13	6	13
Mathematics/mixed	8	11	14	21	20	26	25	30	20	35
Total Mathematics	31	31	36	40	42	37	34	43	26	48
English/arts/social studies	33	31	26	25	24	25	27	17	35	37
English/mixed	3	4	5	14	14	15	14	12	16	20
Total English	36	35	31	39	38	40	41	29	52	58
Geography/arts/social studies	14	13	10	10	10	10	11	11	11	16
Geography/mixed	7	9	8	10	11	11	11	13	9	16
Total Geography	21	23	18	20	21	21	22	25	20	31
Science	33	31	32	28	29	14	13	18	8	18
Arts/social studies	51	48	44	40	39	42	45	35	54	63
Mixed (3)	15	21	24	31	32	44	43	47	38	60
All leavers with two or more A levels/three or more H grades (thousands)										
ENGLAND	86	85	99	99	98	} 123	118	58	60	118
WALES	8	5	6	6	6	}	6	3	4	6
SCOTLAND	.	.	.	17	17	17	16	8	9	16
GREAT BRITAIN	.	.	.	122	121	140	141	69	72	141

(1) See paragraph 13.2 of the explanatory notes.
(2) Due to changes in subject classification, direct comparisons of individual subjects are not possible from 1989/90, with earlier years.
(3) Science and arts or social studies.

TABLE 33[35]:   (i) Students achieving A-level qualifications at school by sex

ENGLAND AND WALES

	Numbers in thousands								As a percentage of total population aged 17 (1)							
	1975/76		1985/86		1989/90		1990/91		1975/76		1985/86		1989/90		1990/91	
	Male	Female	Male	Female	Male	Female	Male	Female	Male	Female	Male	Female	Male	Female	Male	Female
Total population aged 17 (1)	372	352	404	385	369	350	347	327	100	100	100	100	100	100	100	100
From schools only																
3 or more A-level passes	36	24	41	34	45	43	46	45	9.7	6.8	10.2	8.8	12.2	12.3	13.3	13.7
2 A-level passes	15	15	14	15	16	18	15	19	4.0	4.4	3.6	3.8	4.3	5.1	4.3	5.7
1 A-level pass	11	11	11	12	11	12	11	12	2.8	3.2	2.7	3.2	3.0	3.4	3.0	3.6
Total	61	51	67	61	73	73	72	75	16.5	14.4	16.6	15.8	19.8	20.9	20.7	22.9

(ii) Students achieving A-level qualifications at school and through further education (2) by sex

ENGLAND

	Numbers in thousands								As a percentage of total population aged 17 (1)							
	1975/76		1985/86		1989/90		1990/91		1975/76		1985/86		1989/90		1990/91	
	Male	Female	Male	Female	Male	Female	Male	Female	Male	Female	Male	Female	Male	Female	Male	Female
Total population aged 17 (1)	350	335	381	363	348	330	327	308	100	100	100	100	100	100	100	100
From schools and home students from FE colleges aged 19 or less at 31 August	69	59	79	77	82	86	83	88	19.7	17.6	20.6	21.1	23.6	26.1	25.4	28.6
From schools and all students from FE colleges	78	66	87	88	93	103	94	102	..	..	..	..	..	..	..	..

(iii) School leavers achieving SCE H-grade qualifications, by sex

SCOTLAND

	Numbers in thousands								As a percentage of total population aged 16 (1)							
	1975/76		1985/86		1989/90		1990/91		1975/76		1985/86		1989/90		1990/91	
	Male	Female	Male	Female	Male	Female	Male	Female	Male	Female	Male	Female	Male	Female	Male	Female
Total population aged 16 (1)	44	43	43	41	37	35	34	32	100	100	100	100	100	100	100	100
School leavers																
4 or more H-grade passes	6	5	6	7	6	7	6	7	13.6	12.2	14.5	15.9	17.5	20.3	17.6	20.9
3 H-grade passes	2	2	2	2	2	2	2	2	3.9	4.9	4.0	5.5	4.8	6.2	4.7	6.5
2 H-grade passes	2	2	2	3	2	2	2	2	4.0	4.7	4.2	6.1	4.6	6.3	4.6	6.1
1 H-grade pass	2	2	2	3	2	3	2	3	4.5	5.2	5.5	7.3	5.9	8.1	5.8	7.9
Total leavers with H-grade passes	12	12	12	15	12	14	11	13	26.1	27.0	28.2	34.8	32.9	40.9	32.8	41.5

(1) Age at the previous 31 August.

(2) Includes full-time, sandwich and part-time students at FE colleges.

QUALIFICATIONS AND DESTINATIONS

TABLE 34: Students obtaining further education qualifications(1) by subject group and awarding body, 1990/91

Thousands

	Medicine and Dentistry	Allied Medicine	Biological Sciences	Agri-culture and related	Physical Sciences	Mathema-tical and Computing Sciences	Engin-eering and Technology	Archi-tecture, building, planning	Social Studies
AWARDING BODY									
BTEC									
First and National Diploma	0.3	3.4	-	1.5	-	4.5	7.3	3.3	1.5
First and National Certificate	0.1	1.3	-	0.1	0.1	2.0	21.6	6.7	1.6
TOTAL	0.4	4.7	-	1.5	0.1	6.5	28.8	10.0	3.1
CGLI (2),(3)									
All awards & Certificates	0.1	1.0	-	18.5	1.0	11.0	107.2	87.6	8.2

(1) Excluding 134,465 students taking the SCOTVEC National Certificate. Also excludes other further education qualifications awarded by other bodies (e.g RSA, LCCI).

(2) Subject split has been estimated based on subject distribution of enrolments for England.

(3) Excluding 17.8 thousand Armed Forces examination awards.

TABLE 34(continued):   Students obtaining further education qualifications(1) by subject group and awarding body

Thousands

	Business and admin studies	Communi-cation and Docum-entation	Langu-ages and related	Human-ities	Creative Arts and design	Educ-ation	Combined and General	ALL STUDENTS	MALES	FEMALES
AWARDING BODY										
BTEC										
First and National Diploma	26.3	0.1	-	-	14.3	-	5.6	68.1	35.1	33.0
First and National Certificate	15.4	-	-	-	0.6	-	2.5	51.9	33.9	18.0
TOTAL	41.7	0.1	-	-	14.8	-	8.1	120.0	69.0	51.0
CGLI (2),(3)										
All awards & Certificates	47.4	2.1	2.1	-	42.2	11.7	3.4	343.5	255.5	87.9

See previous page for footnotes

QUALIFICATIONS AND DESTINATIONS

TABLE 35[36]: Students obtaining higher education qualifications by subject of study(1)(2), sex and type of awarding body, 1989/90(3)

Thousands

	Medicine and Dentistry	Allied Medicine	Biological Sciences	Agri-culture and related	Physical Sciences	Mathema-tical and Computing Sciences	Engin-eering and Technology	Archi-tecture, building, planning	Social Studies
PERSONS									
Higher Degree Level									
University	1.4	0.9	2.2	0.7	2.6	1.9	4.1	0.6	4.7
CNAA	-	0.1	0.2	0.0	0.2	0.3	0.5	0.1	0.2
Open University (4)	..	..	..	..	..	..	..	..	..
Professional Qualifications (5)	-	0.1	-	-	-	-	0.3	0.4	0.1
Total Higher Degree Level	1.4	1.1	2.4	0.7	2.9	2.3	4.9	1.2	5.1
Higher Diplomas and Certificates									
University (6)(7)	0.6	0.4	0.2	0.1	0.2	0.3	0.4	0.3	1.9
CNAA (6)	-	0.1	-	-	-	0.3	0.2	0.1	0.2
Total Higher Diplomas and Certificates	0.6	0.5	0.2	0.1	0.2	0.6	0.6	0.4	2.1
First Degree Level									
University	5.6	2.2	5.7	1.3	6.5	4.6	9.8	1.4	11.9
CNAA	-	1.4	1.4	0.1	2.2	2.5	6.1	2.6	7.4
University validated degrees (7)	-	-	0.1	-	0.2	0.1	-	-	0.2
Open University (4)	..	..	..	..	..	..	..	..	..
Professional Qualifications (5)	-	-	-	-	0.2	0.4	1.1	0.9	0.9
Total First Degree Level (7)	5.6	3.6	7.2	1.4	9.0	7.6	16.9	4.9	20.3
Sub-degree Level									
First university diplomas and certificates (7)(8)	0.1	0.2	0.2	-	0.2	0.3	0.4	0.2	0.8
CNAA diplomas and certificates (9)	-	0.3	0.2	-	0.1	-	-	-	0.5
Professional qualifications (5)	-	4.1	-	0.2	0.3	0.7	1.8	2.7	4.1
BTEC higher diploma	-	0.1	0.4	0.6	0.5	2.8	4.1	0.9	0.2
BTEC higher certificate	-	0.5	0.3	0.1	1.0	1.3	10.9	3.7	0.9
SCOTVEC higher diploma/certificate	-	-	0.1	0.1	0.1	0.3	0.5	0.1	-
Total Sub-degree Level	0.1	5.2	1.2	1.0	2.2	5.4	17.7	7.5	6.6
Nursing and Paramedical courses	.	30.8	.	.	.	.	.	.	.
TOTAL HIGHER EDUCATION 1990	7.7	41.2	11.0	3.2	14.2	16.0	40.2	14.0	34.1
TOTAL HIGHER EDUCATION 1989	7.6	40.1	10.1	3.3	13.8	15.1	37.4	11.7	32.2
TOTAL HIGHER EDUCATION 1979 (2)(11)	..	..	..	..	..	..	..	..	..
MALES									
Higher degree level	0.8	0.5	1.4	0.5	2.3	1.7	4.3	0.9	2.9
Higher diplomas and certificates	0.3	0.1	0.1	0.1	0.2	0.5	0.6	0.2	1.1
First degree level(7)	3.1	1.1	3.1	0.8	6.4	5.8	15.3	4.0	9.9
Sub-degree level	0.1	1.2	0.7	0.6	1.5	3.6	13.3	5.4	2.8
Nursing and Paramedical courses	.	2.8	.	.	.	.	.	.	.
FEMALES									
Higher degree level	0.6	0.5	1.0	0.2	0.6	0.5	0.5	0.3	2.1
Higher diplomas and certificates	0.2	0.4	0.1	-	0.1	0.1	0.1	0.1	1.0
First degree level(7)	2.5	2.6	4.1	0.6	2.6	1.8	1.6	0.9	10.4
Sub-degree level	0.1	4.0	0.5	0.3	0.7	1.8	4.5	2.1	3.8
Nursing and Paramedical courses	.	28.0	.	.	.	.	.	.	.

(1) Teacher training results are shown in Table 8. However, these overlap with results shown here.

(2) Due to changes in subject classification in 1987/88, a comparable subject split of the qualifications for earlier years is not available.

(3) Excluding qualifications from the private sector. University diplomas and certificates relate to the calendar year 1990.

(4) Open Unversity degrees subject detail is not available in this format. Included only in "All students", "Males" and "Females" totals.

(5) Public sector only. DFE estimates based on final year of course data.

(6) Including Postgraduate Certificates in Education (PGCE's).

TABLE 35[36]: Students obtaining higher education qualifications by subject of study(1)(2), sex and type of awarding body, 1989/90(3)

Thousands

	Business and admin studies	Communi-cation and Docum-entation	Langu-ages and related	Human-ities	Creative Arts and design	Edu-cation	Combined and General	All Students	Males	Females
PERSONS										
Higher Degree Level										
University	4.3	0.4	1.8	1.5	0.3	3.2	0.6	31.4	20.9	10.5
CNAA	0.7	0.2	-	0.1	0.3	0.2	-	3.3	2.3	1.1
Open University (4)	..	..	..	..	..	..	..	0.7	0.3	0.4
Professional Qualifications (5)	0.4	0.1	-	-	0.2	-	-	1.6	1.0	0.6
Total Higher Degree Level	5.4	0.7	1.8	1.6	0.8	3.4	0.7	37.0	24.5	12.5
Higher Diplomas and Certificates										
University (6)(7)	1.0	0.4	0.2	0.2	0.2	6.8	0.1	13.2	6.1	7.1
CNAA (6)	1.0	0.5	-	0.1	0.2	4.6	-	7.3	2.9	4.4
Total Higher Diplomas and Certificates	2.0	0.8	0.2	0.3	0.3	11.5	0.1	20.5	8.9	11.6
First Degree Level										
University	3.9	0.1	7.7	5.2	1.5	1.4	8.6	77.2	43.3	33.9
CNAA	7.7	0.8	1.4	0.4	6.5	4.8	7.2	52.5	27.6	24.9
University validated degrees (7)	0.1	0.1	0.4	0.2	0.5	1.3	2.7	5.9	1.5	4.4
Open University (4)	..	..	..	..	..	..	..	6.5	3.3	3.2
Professional Qualifications - Level 6 (5)	5.2	0.2	0.3	-	0.4	-	0.2	9.8	6.1	3.8
Total First Degree Level (7)	16.9	1.2	9.8	5.8	8.9	7.5	18.7	151.9	81.8	70.1
Sub-degree Level										
First university diplomas and certificates (7)(8)	0.6	-	0.8	0.4	0.3	0.5	2.9	7.8	3.4	4.4
CNAA diplomas and certificates (9)	2.9 (10)	-	0.4	0.7	0.5	4.9	-	10.6	5.3	5.3
Professional qualifications (5)	23.4	0.5	0.8	0.1	0.6	0.8	0.9	41.1	20.3	20.8
BTEC higher diploma	8.0	-	-	-	2.9	-	0.2	20.6	12.9	7.7
BTEC higher certificate	4.6	-	-	-	0.1	-	0.1	23.5	17.8	5.7
SCOTVEC higher diploma/certificate	1.8	0.2	-	-	0.2	-	-	3.5	1.7	1.7
Total Sub-degree Level	41.4	0.7	2.0	1.2	4.5	6.2	4.1	107.1	61.6	45.5
Nursing and Paramedical courses	.	.	.	.	.	.	.	30.8	2.8	28.0
TOTAL HIGHER EDUCATION 1990	65.7	3.5	13.8	8.9	14.6	28.6	23.6	347.2	179.5	167.7
TOTAL HIGHER EDUCATION 1989	55.8	3.2	14.1	8.6	12.8	26.8	21.4	322.4	169.5	152.9
TOTAL HIGHER EDUCATION 1979 (2)(11)	..	..	..	..	..	..	..	213.0	143.0	69.0
MALES										
Higher degree level	3.8	0.3	0.8	1.0	0.4	1.7	0.4	.	24.5	.
Higher diplomas and certificates	1.0	0.3	0.1	0.1	0.2	4.0	0.1	.	8.9	.
First degree level(7)	9.2	0.4	2.8	3.0	3.5	1.9	8.3	.	81.8	.
Sub-degree level	24.2	0.3	0.6	0.6	2.6	2.6	1.6	.	61.6	.
Nursing and Paramedical courses	.	.	.	.	.	.	.	.	2.8	.
FEMALES										
Higher degree level	1.6	0.4	1.0	0.6	0.4	1.7	0.3	.	.	12.5
Higher diplomas and certificates	1.0	0.5	0.1	0.1	0.2	7.5	-	.	.	11.6
First degree level(7)	7.7	0.8	7.0	2.8	5.4	5.6	10.5	.	.	70.1
Sub-degree level	17.2	0.5	1.4	0.7	2.0	3.6	2.5	.	.	45.5
Nursing and Paramedical courses	.	.	.	.	.	.	.	.	.	28.0

(7) DFE estimates based on various sources. Total first degrees include a small number of conversion courses.

(8) Excluding students who successfully completed courses for which formal qualifications are not awarded.

(9) Including Dip HE and Certificates of Education.

(10) Including Diploma in Management Studies, which is equivalent to First degree.

(11) Excluding University validated degrees and nursing and paramedic qualifiers.

QUALIFICATIONS AND DESTINATIONS

Table 36[37]: First destinations of first degree graduates at 31 December 1991 by sex and subject group

(i) First degree graduates - All destinations - From academic year 1990/91

Thousands

	UK EMPLOYMENT		Overseas employment	Further education/ training	Believed unemployed	Other(2)	Unknown	Total
	Permanent (1) employment	Temporary employment						
MALES								
Medicine and Dentistry	2.1	-	-	0.1	-	-	0.1	2.4
Studies allied to medicine	0.7	-	-	0.1	-	-	0.1	1.0
Biological sciences	0.7	0.2	-	1.1	0.4	0.2	0.3	3.0
Vet. science, agriculture etc	0.4	-	-	0.1	0.1	0.1	0.1	0.7
Physical sciences	1.6	0.3	0.1	2.2	0.7	0.4	0.6	5.9
Mathematical sciences	2.6	0.2	0.1	1.0	0.9	0.5	0.7	6.0
Engineering and technology	5.8	0.4	0.2	1.9	1.4	2.4	1.5	13.6
Architecture etc	1.3	0.1	0.1	0.3	0.4	0.3	0.4	2.8
Social sciences	2.5	0.5	0.2	2.9	1.0	1.3	1.4	9.7
Business and financial studies	2.9	0.3	0.1	0.5	0.8	0.9	0.8	6.4
Librarianship & info. sciences	0.1	-	-	-	0.1	-	-	0.3
Languages	0.7	0.2	0.2	0.7	0.3	0.2	0.5	2.8
Humanities	0.8	0.1	0.1	0.8	0.4	0.2	0.5	3.0
Creative Arts	1.2	0.2	0.1	0.5	0.5	0.3	1.0	3.7
Education	0.7	0.1	-	0.1	0.1	0.1	0.2	1.2
Multi-disciplinary studies	2.6	0.5	0.2	1.7	1.2	0.8	1.6	8.6
All subjects	26.7	3.1	1.5	14.1	8.2	7.8	9.7	71.1
FEMALES								
Medicine and Dentistry	1.9	-	-	-	-	-	0.1	2.0
Studies allied to medicine	2.0	0.1	-	0.2	0.1	0.1	0.2	2.7
Biological sciences	1.3	0.2	0.1	1.3	0.3	0.3	0.3	3.9
Vet. science, agriculture etc	0.3	-	-	0.1	0.1	0.1	0.1	0.6
Physical sciences	0.9	0.2	0.1	0.9	0.3	0.2	0.2	2.7
Mathematical sciences	0.9	0.1	-	0.4	0.2	0.2	0.2	2.1
Engineering and technology	0.8	0.1	-	0.2	0.1	0.3	0.1	1.6
Architecture etc	0.4	0.1	-	0.2	0.1	0.1	0.1	0.9
Social sciences	2.7	0.6	0.2	3.3	0.8	1.2	1.4	10.2
Business and financial studies	2.9	0.4	0.2	0.5	0.5	0.8	0.7	6.0
Librarianship & info. sciences	0.3	0.1	-	0.1	0.1	0.1	0.1	0.8
Languages	2.1	0.5	0.7	1.9	0.6	0.6	0.8	7.2
Humanities	1.0	0.2	0.1	0.8	0.3	0.3	0.4	3.2
Creative Arts	1.8	0.3	0.1	0.9	0.6	0.4	1.2	5.4
Education	3.2	0.1	-	0.1	0.1	0.2	0.4	4.2
Multi-disciplinary studies	3.7	0.8	0.4	2.6	1.1	0.9	1.8	11.3
All subjects	26.1	3.6	1.9	13.8	5.3	6.0	8.1	64.7
PERSONS								
Medicine and Dentistry	4.0	-	-	0.1	-	0.1	0.2	4.4
Studies allied to medicine	2.7	0.1	-	0.4	0.1	0.2	0.2	3.7
Biological sciences	2.0	0.4	0.1	2.4	0.7	0.6	0.6	6.9
Vet. science, agriculture etc	0.7	-	-	0.2	0.1	0.1	0.2	1.4
Physical sciences	2.5	0.5	0.2	3.1	1.0	0.5	0.8	8.5
Mathematical sciences	3.6	0.3	0.1	1.5	1.0	0.7	0.9	8.0
Engineering and technology	6.6	0.4	0.2	2.2	1.5	2.6	1.6	15.2
Architecture etc	1.6	0.2	0.1	0.5	0.5	0.4	0.5	3.8
Social sciences	5.2	1.1	0.3	6.2	1.8	2.5	2.7	19.9
Business and financial studies	5.8	0.7	0.3	1.1	1.3	1.7	1.5	12.4
Librarianship & info. sciences	0.5	0.1	-	0.1	0.1	0.1	0.1	1.1
Languages	2.7	0.6	1.0	2.6	1.0	0.9	1.3	10.0
Humanities	1.9	0.3	0.2	1.6	0.7	0.5	0.9	6.2
Creative Arts	3.0	0.5	0.2	1.4	1.1	0.7	2.2	9.1
Education	3.9	0.2	0.1	0.2	0.2	0.4	0.6	5.4
Multi-disciplinary studies	6.2	1.3	0.6	4.3	2.4	1.7	3.4	19.9
All subjects	52.8	6.8	3.5	27.8	13.5	13.8	17.8	135.9
Total all subjects								
1990/91	52.8	6.8	3.5	27.8	13.5	13.8	17.8	135.9
1989/90(3)	55.9	5.6	3.0	22.3	8.8	11.8	16.8	124.2
1985/86(3)	55.7	3.5	2.4	20.9	8.2	6.4	15.2	112.4
1980/81(4)	..	..	..	..	..	..	..	91.9

(1) Includes those remaining with or returning to a previous employer.
(2) Includes overseas graduates leaving UK and graduates not available for employment.
(3) Great Britain.
(4) Due to revisions in the format it is not possible to provide detailed breakdown for 1980/81.

Table 36[37]:   First destinations of first degree graduates at 31 December 1991 by sex and subject group

(ii) Employment categories of first degree graduates known to have entered permanent home employment (1) - 1990/91

Thousands

	Admin. Management services	Scientific, Engineering	Marketing	Financial, Legal	Personnel, Medical Social	Teaching, Lecturing	Other and unknown (2)	Total entered permanent employment
MALES								
Medicine and Dentistry	-	-	-	-	2.1	-	-	2.1
Studies allied to medicine	-	-	-	-	0.6	-	-	0.7
Biological sciences	0.1	0.3	0.1	0.1	0.1	-	0.1	0.7
Vet. science, agriculture etc	0.1	0.1	-	-	0.1	-	-	0.4
Physical sciences	0.3	0.7	0.1	0.2	0.1	-	0.2	1.6
Mathematical sciences	1.6	0.2	0.1	0.4	-	0.1	0.2	2.6
Engineering and technology	0.7	4.3	0.1	0.2	0.1	-	0.4	5.8
Architecture etc	0.1	1.0	-	-	-	-	0.1	1.3
Social sciences	0.4	0.1	0.3	0.8	0.3	0.1	0.5	2.5
Business and financial studies	0.6	0.2	0.5	1.4	0.1	-	0.3	2.9
Librarianship & info. sciences	-	-	-	-	-	-	0.1	0.1
Languages	0.1	-	0.1	0.1	-	0.1	0.2	0.7
Humanities	0.1	-	0.1	0.1	0.1	0.1	0.3	0.8
Creative Arts	0.1	0.1	-	-	-	0.2	0.7	1.2
Education	-	-	-	-	-	0.5	0.2	0.7
Multi-disciplinary studies	0.5	0.2	0.3	0.6	0.2	0.2	0.5	2.6
All subjects	4.7	7.2	1.7	4.1	3.9	1.3	3.8	26.7
FEMALES								
Medicine and Dentistry	-	-	-	-	1.8	-	-	1.9
Studies allied to medicine	-	0.1	-	-	1.8	-	0.1	2.0
Biological sciences	0.1	0.5	0.1	0.1	0.2	0.1	0.2	1.3
Vet. science, agriculture etc	0.1	0.1	-	-	0.1	-	-	0.3
Physical sciences	0.1	0.4	0.1	0.1	0.1	0.1	0.1	0.9
Mathematical sciences	0.4	0.1	-	0.2	-	0.1	0.1	0.9
Engineering and technology	0.1	0.5	-	-	-	-	0.1	0.8
Architecture etc	-	0.3	-	-	-	-	-	0.4
Social sciences	0.4	-	0.2	0.5	0.7	0.2	0.5	2.7
Business and financial studies	0.7	0.1	0.5	1.0	0.1	0.1	0.3	2.9
Librarianship & info. sciences	0.1	-	-	-	-	-	0.2	0.3
Languages	0.4	-	0.3	0.2	0.1	0.4	0.6	2.1
Humanities	0.2	-	0.1	0.1	0.1	0.2	0.3	1.0
Creative Arts	0.1	-	0.1	-	0.1	0.4	1.1	1.8
Education	-	-	-	-	-	2.7	0.4	3.2
Multi-disciplinary studies	0.6	0.2	0.4	0.5	0.4	0.6	0.9	3.7
All subjects	3.3	2.2	2.0	2.8	5.7	5.1	5.0	26.1
PERSONS								
Medicine and Dentistry	-	-	-	-	3.9	-	-	4.0
Studies allied to medicine	-	0.1	-	-	2.4	0.1	0.1	2.7
Biological sciences	0.2	0.8	0.2	0.2	0.3	0.1	0.3	2.0
Vet. science, agriculture etc	0.2	0.1	-	-	0.2	-	0.1	0.7
Physical sciences	0.4	1.1	0.1	0.3	0.1	0.1	0.3	2.5
Mathematical sciences	1.9	0.3	0.1	0.7	0.1	0.2	0.3	3.6
Engineering and technology	0.8	4.8	0.2	0.2	0.1	-	0.5	6.6
Architecture etc	0.1	1.3	-	-	-	-	0.1	1.6
Social sciences	0.8	0.1	0.5	1.3	1.0	0.3	1.1	5.2
Business and financial studies	1.3	0.3	1.0	2.3	0.2	0.2	0.6	5.8
Librarianship & info. sciences	0.1	-	0.1	-	-	-	0.3	0.5
Languages	0.5	-	0.4	0.3	0.2	0.5	0.8	2.7
Humanities	0.3	-	0.2	0.2	0.2	0.3	0.6	1.9
Creative Arts	0.1	0.1	0.1	-	0.1	0.7	1.9	3.0
Education	0.1	-	-	-	0.1	3.2	0.6	3.9
Multi-disciplinary studies	1.2	0.4	0.7	1.1	0.6	0.8	1.4	6.2
All subjects	7.9	9.5	3.7	6.9	9.6	6.4	8.8	52.8
Total all subjects								
1990/91	8.0	9.5	3.7	6.9	9.6	6.4	8.8	52.8
1989/90(3)	8.7	12.3	4.1	8.4	9.5	5.8	7.2	55.9
1985/86(3),(4)	9.1	11.1	4.5	9.4	9.1	5.0	6.9	54.9
1980/81(5)	..	..	..	..	..	..	..	36.1

(1) Includes those remaining with or returning to a previous employer.

(2) Includes overseas graduates leaving UK and graduates not available for employment.

(3) Great Britain.

(4) Excludes university graduates remaining with or returning to a previous employer.

(5) Due to revisions in the format it is not possible to provide detailed breakdown for 1980/81.

QUALIFICATIONS AND DESTINATIONS

TABLE 37[38]:   Highest qualification held by people aged 16-59 by sex and economic activity 1991

UNITED KINGDOM	PERSONS		MALES		FEMALES	
	All	Econ Active(1)	All	Econ Active(1)	All	Econ Active(1)
NUMBERS (thousands)	32,608	26,379	16,366	14,822	16,242	11,557
PERCENTAGE	100	100	100	100	100	100
HIGHEST QUALIFICATION (Percentage)						
Degree or equivalent	9	10	11	11	6	7
Higher degree	1	2	2	2	1	1
First degree	6	7	7	7	5	6
Member of professional institution	1	1	2	2	1	1
Higher Education below degree level	6	7	5	5	7	8
HNC/HND/BEC(Higher)/TEC(Higher)	3	3	4	4	1	1
Teaching: Further education	-	-	-	-	-	-
Teaching: Secondary	-	-	-	-	1	1
Teaching: Primary	1	1	-	-	1	1
Nursing qualification	2	2	-	-	4	4
GCE A Level or equivalent	26	28	35	35	16	17
ONC/OND/BEC(NatGen)TEC(NatGen)	3	3	4	4	2	3
City and Guilds	9	10	14	15	4	4
A Level or equivalent	7	7	7	7	7	8
Trade apprenticeship completed	6	7	10	10	3	3
O Level or equivalent	19	19	15	15	24	25
CSE below Grade 1	4	4	4	4	5	5
YTS certificate	-	-	-	-	-	-
Other Qualification	6	6	5	5	7	7
No qualification	30	26	25	24	34	29
Non respondents	1	1	1	1	1	1

(1) The economically active is defined as those in employment plus the unemployed (ILO definition).

TABLE 38[39]: Highest qualification held by people aged 16-59, by age and sex 1991

UNITED KINGDOM

PERSONS

AGE GROUPS	16-59	16-24	25-29	30-39	40-49	50-59
NUMBERS (thousands)	32,608	7,118	4,566	7,710	7,418	5,796
PERCENTAGE	100	100	100	100	100	100

HIGHEST QUALIFICATION (Percentage)

	16-59	16-24	25-29	30-39	40-49	50-59
Degree or equivalent	9	3	11	12	10	6
Higher Education below degree level	6	3	7	7	7	6
GCE A Level or equivalent	26	29	28	27	24	21
O Level or equivalent	19	33	23	18	13	8
Other qualification(1)	10	10	12	10	10	10
No qualification	30	21	18	26	35	47
Other(2)	1	1	1	1	1	1

MALES

AGE GROUPS	16-59	16-24	25-29	30-39	40-49	50-59
NUMBERS (thousands)	16,366	3,618	2,302	3,866	3,708	2,872
PERCENTAGE	100	100	100	100	100	100

HIGHEST QUALIFICATION (Percentage)

	16-59	16-24	25-29	30-39	40-49	50-59
Degree or equivalent	11	4	13	15	14	9
Higher Education below degree level	5	3	6	6	6	5
GCE A Level or equivalent	35	32	36	38	35	33
O Level or equivalent	15	29	16	11	9	6
Other qualification(1)	9	9	11	8	8	9
No qualification	25	23	18	21	28	37
Other(2)	1	1	1	1	1	1

FEMALES

AGE GROUPS	16-59	16-24	25-29	30-39	40-49	50-59
NUMBERS (thousands)	16,242	3,500	2,265	3,844	3,709	2,924
PERCENTAGE	100	100	100	100	100	100

HIGHEST QUALIFICATION (Percentage)

	16-59	16-24	25-29	30-39	40-49	50-59
Degree or equivalent	6	3	9	10	6	3
Higher Education below degree level	7	3	8	8	8	8
GCE A Level or equivalent	16	25	20	16	13	9
O Level or equivalent	24	37	31	24	17	11
Other qualification(1)	12	11	13	11	12	12
No qualification	34	20	19	30	43	57
Other(2)	1	1	-	-	1	1

(1) Includes CSE below grade 1, YTS certificate, other qualifications.

(2) Includes unknowns and non respondents.

QUALIFICATIONS AND DESTINATIONS

TABLE 39[40]: Highest qualification held by people aged 16-59 by sex and broad age group 1984 and 1991

UNITED KINGDOM

PERSONS

AGE GROUPS	16-59		16-29		30-59	
YEAR	1984	1991	1984	1991	1984	1991
NUMBERS (thousands)	31,626	32,608	11,768	11,685	19,858	20,923
PERCENTAGE	100	100	100	100	100	100
HIGHEST QUALIFICATION (Percentage)						
Degree or equivalent	7	9	5	6	8	10
Higher Education below degree level	6	6	4	4	7	7
GCE A Level or equivalent	22	26	23	28	21	24
O Level or equivalent	16	19	26	29	10	14
Other qualification(1)	9	10	13	11	6	10
No qualification	39	30	27	20	47	35
Other(2)	2	1	1	1	2	1

MALES

AGE GROUPS	16-59		16-29		30-59	
YEAR	1984	1991	1984	1991	1984	1991
NUMBERS (thousands)	15,862	16,366	5,955	5,920	9,907	10,446
PERCENTAGE	100	100	100	100	100	100
HIGHEST QUALIFICATION (Percentage)						
Degree or equivalent	9	11	6	7	11	13
Higher Education below degree level	4	5	3	4	5	6
GCE A Level or equivalent	31	35	31	33	32	35
O Level or equivalent	12	15	21	24	7	9
Other qualification(1)	7	9	11	10	4	8
No qualification	34	25	27	21	39	28
Other(2)	2	1	2	1	2	1

FEMALES

AGE GROUPS	16-59		16-29		30-59	
YEAR	1984	1991	1984	1991	1984	1991
NUMBERS (thousands)	15,764	16,242	5,813	5,765	9,952	10,477
PERCENTAGE	100	100	100	100	100	100
HIGHEST QUALIFICATION (Percentage)						
Degree or equivalent	4	6	5	6	4	7
Higher Education below degree level	7	7	4	5	8	8
GCE A Level or equivalent	12	16	16	23	9	13
O Level or equivalent	20	24	31	35	13	18
Other qualification(1)	11	12	15	12	8	12
No qualification	45	34	27	19	55	42
Other(2)	2	1	1	1	2	1

(1) Includes CSE below grade 1, YTS certificate (for 1991 only), other qualifications.

(2) Includes unknowns and non respondents.

SOURCES OF UNITED KINGDOM EDUCATION STATISTICS

1. GENERAL SOURCES

1.1   Various summaries of statistics for all four parts of the United Kingdom, and for universities both in Great Britain and Northern Ireland are contained in the Annual Abstract of Statistics, Regional Trends and Social Trends prepared by the Central Statistical Office. Some education statistics also appear in the Digest of Welsh Statistics, the Scottish Abstract of Statistics (which has superseded the former Digest of Scottish Statistics) and the Digest of Statistics, Northern Ireland.

1.2   For the period 1966 to 1979, Her Majesty's Stationery Office published annually a series of "Statistics of Education" volumes, each relating to a particular subject or subjects. Volumes 1 to 5 ceased to be published by HMSO after the 1979 series became available, and for 1980 onwards a new series of volumes has been published by the Department For Education (DFE). Volume 6 also ceased after 1979 and was replaced by three publications covering Students and Staff, First Destinations of University Graduates and Finance. Details of how to obtain copies of these new volumes are shown inside the back cover, together with information on other publications.

1.3   In July 1978 the Department For Education introduced a new series of Statistical Bulletins. To date about 240 have been produced. These are issued primarily to make available quickly key educational statistics (including provisional figures and estimates) in advance of their production in the "Statistics of Education" volumes. A secondary purpose of the bulletins is to announce the production of each volume and to present a sample of its contents. Bulletins are also issued to disseminate information on other topics of statistical interest. From 1977, the Scottish Education Department replaced their Scottish Educational Statistics by a series of Statistical Bulletins, of which about 184 have been published.

The DFE titles below include only the latest annual and periodic Bulletins. Previous editions of this publication include a list of pre–1991 Bulletins, some of which will be of historical/topical interest.

NO	TITLES
1/91	School Examinations Survey 1988/89
2/91	Mature Students in Higher Education – 1975 to 1988
3/91	Education Statistics for the United Kingdom 1990 Edition
4/91	Student Awards in England and Wales: 1988–89
5/91	Pupil/Teacher ratios for each Local Education Authority in England (including Grant Maintained Schools) – January 1990

6/91	Independent Schools in England – January 1990
7/91	Pupils under Five Years in each Local Education Authority in England – January 1990
8/91	Student/Staff ratios and Unit Costs at Higher and Further Education Establishments in England
9/91	Statistics of Schools in England – January 1990
10/91	Student Numbers in Higher Education – Great Britain 1979 to 1989
11/91	Survey of Information Technology in School
12/91	Survey of Information Technology in Initial Teacher Training
13/91	Educational & Economic Activity of Young People aged 16 to 18 years in England from 1974/75 to 1989/90
14/91	Participation in Education by Young People aged 16 and 17 in each Local Education Authority & Region; England 1985/86 to 1989/90
15/91	First Known Destination of First Degree Graduates from Institutions in Great Britain 1963–1989
16/91	Students in Higher Education in England excluding universities
17/91	Students on Initial Teacher Training Courses
18/91	Secondary School Staffing Survey – 1988
19/91	Statistics of Further Education Students in England 1970/71 – 1989/90
20/91	Students from Abroad in Great Britain 1980 to 1989
21/91	Education Expenditure from 1979–80
22/91	School Examinations Survey 1989/90
1/92	Teachers in Service and Teacher vacancies in England in January 1991
2/92	Pupil/teacher ratios for each local education authority in England (including grant–maintained schools) – January 1991
3/92	Education statistics for the United Kingdom 1991
4/92	First known destinations of First Degree Graduates from institutions in Great Britain 1983–1990
5/92	Pupils under 5 years in each Local Education Authority in England – January 1991
6/92	Student Awards in England and Wales: 1989/90

7/92	Student Loans 1990/91
8/92	Students in Higher Education in Great Britain
9/92	Leaving rates amongst First Year Degree Students in English Polytechnics and Colleges
10/92	Education Expenditure from 1979–80
11/92	Student: staff ratios and unit costs at Higher and Further Education establishments outside Universities in England
12/92	Students on Initial Teacher Training Courses
13/92	Statistics of Schools in England – January 1991
14/92	Participation in Education by 16–18 year olds in England from 1979/80 to 1991/92
15/92	School Examination Survey 1990/91
16/92	Participation in Education by young people aged 16 and 17 in each Local Education Authority and region of England: 1988/89 to 1990/91
17/92	Statistics of Further Education Students in England 1970/71 to 1990/91
18/92	Mature students in Higher Education – Great Britain 1980 to 1990
19/92	Students in Higher Education – England 1990

2.   CSO PUBLICATIONS

The Central Statistical Office publishes a quarterly journal entitled "Statistical News" (price £5.50) which contains short articles and notes on the latest developments in all fields of government statistics, including education.

"Social Trends" is produced annually, No 23 1993 (price £26.00) being the current edition. This publication brings together some of the more significant statistical series relating to social policies and conditions and presents a series of articles, followed by tables and charts. One chapter concentrates on education.

"Regional Trends" is also published annually, No 27 1992 (price £24.75) being the current edition. This publication brings together detailed information highlighting regional variations in the United Kingdom and covering a wide range of social, demographic and economic topics. One chapter concentrates on education.

"A Guide to Official Statistics" No 5 (Revised 1990) (price £24.00) sets out to give the user a broad indication of the range of government statistics available and, if so, the publication in which they appear.

3. EDUCATIONAL REPORTS

A number of important education reports of recent years contain statistical tables and results of special surveys. They are set out below. Previous editions of this publication include a list of pre–1986 reports.

Managing Colleges Efficiently – a study of efficiency in non–advanced further education for the Government and Local Authority Associations. HMSO, 1987. £3.95. ISBN 0 11 270626 6.

Mature Students' Incomings and Outgoings Survey. HMSO, 1987. £11.50. ISBN 0 11 691269 3.

Non Advanced Further Education in Practice. HMSO, 1987. £4.50. ISBN 0 11 270609 6.

Catching Up? National Bureau for Handicapped Students, 1987.

Undergraduate Income and Expenditure Survey. Research Services Ltd, 1987.

Projected Numbers of Students in Maintained Colleges studying on Non–advanced courses, England 1986 – 2000. DFE, 1988.

Education in Britain. Central Office of Information, 1989.

International Statistical Comparisons in Higher Education Working Report. DFE, 1990.

Highly Qualified People: Supply and Demand: Report of an Interdepartmental Review. HMSO, 1990. £6.90. ISBN 0 11 270713 0.

An Overview of the Demand for Graduates. HMSO, 1990. £6.50. ISBN 0 11 270712 2.

Projecting the Supply and Demand of Teachers: a Technical Description. HMSO, 1990. £10.50. ISBN 0 11 270745 9.

Education and Training for the 21st Century. (CM 1536) HMSO, 1991. £11.00. ISBN 0 10 115362 7.

Higher Education: a New Framework. (CM 1541) HMSO, 1991. £6.60. ISBN 0 10 115412 7.

Testing 7 Year Olds in 1991: Results of the National Curriculum assessments in England. DFE, 1992

Education at a Glance: OECD Indicators. Organisation for Economic Co-operation and Development. HMSO, 1992. £16. ISBN 926403692X.

School Performance Tables: Public Examination Results 1992. DFE, 1992.

Testing 7 Year Olds in 1992: Results of the National Curriculum assessments in England. DFE 1992.

Testing 14 Year Olds in 1992: Results of the National Curriculum assessments in England. DFE 1992.

EXPLANATORY NOTES

GENERAL

Differences in the way that the statistics are returned or recorded by the contributors have been mentioned in the explanatory notes or footnotes where they are considered to be significant. For reasons of space it is impracticable to identify all the differences.

1. GEOGRAPHIC COVERAGE

1.1   For statistical purposes the United Kingdom is England, Wales, Scotland and Northern Ireland. Great Britain excludes Northern Ireland. Statistics for the Isle of Man and the Channel Islands are not included in this publication. Tables show summary data for individual countries as far as possible, but not where data have been estimated for them.

1.2   The following is a brief account of the education system as it operates in the United Kingdom. It ignores many detailed aspects in order to give a general picture.

2. STRUCTURE, ADMINISTRATION AND METHOD

2.1   United Kingdom educational establishments are administered and financed in one of three ways:

a.   by local education authorities (LEAs)(l), which form part of the structure of local government partly through funds provided by central government;

b.   by governing bodies, which have a substantial degree of autonomy from public authorities but which receive grants from centrally financed funding bodies and from central government sources directly;

c.   by the private sector, including individuals, companies and charitable institutions.

---

(1)   Corresponding to counties, metropolitan districts, the Inner and Outer London Boroughs. Most local education authorities in England and Wales had their boundaries redrawn with effect from 1 April 1974 and those in Scotland from 16 May 1975. From 1 October 1973, the 8 local education authorities in Northern Ireland were replaced by 5 Education and Library Boards.

2.2   Types of establishments falling within the categories typically have different names in England, Wales, Scotland and Northern Ireland. Therefore, to avoid confusion, standardised terms are used for the purposes of United Kingdom statistics:

a.   Public sector –   maintained and grant–maintained (England and Wales)

assisted and grant–aided establishments of further education (England and Wales)

education authority (Scotland)

controlled, maintained, voluntary and grant–maintained integrated (Northern Ireland)

b.   Part–maintained –   grant–aided (Scotland) until 1985/86

direct grant (England and Wales) until 1980

c.   Non–maintained –   independent (see paragraph 10.6 also)

With effect from 30 October 1980, all direct grant schools in England and Wales became independent. Likewise, from 1985/86, all but twelve of the Scottish grant aided schools became independent, the remainder staying grant maintained. In the tables of this volume, the non–maintained sector generally includes the part–maintained establishments throughout the whole of the time series shown, unless the footnotes states otherwise. The term "public school" as commonly used in the United Kingdom is now a misnomer. It refers for historical reasons to certain of the major independent schools.

2.3   In general the education services of the United Kingdom are not subject to detailed central control. Standards are maintained by an Inspectorate having access to all institutions except the universities (other than for teacher training) and related bodies. Within this framework, detailed control is exercised by local education authorities or by various forms of independent governing bodies, in association with the teaching staff. In all sectors, such matters as engaging teachers, teaching methods and selection of textbooks are part of these detailed local responsibilities.

Some central control is, however, exercised over the curriculum taught during compulsory schooling. In particular, the Education Reform Act 1988 introduced the National Curriculum in England and Wales which includes the core subjects of English, mathematics and science (Welsh in Wales) and seven (eight in Wales) other foundation subjects. The 1988 Act also provided for local authorities to delegate the management of school budgets to the schools themselves and for schools to seek withdrawal from LEA control and become grant–maintained.

2.4   The four home Government Departments responsible for education are:

a.   **Department For Education** (known as Department of Education and Science prior to 6 July 1992):   all sectors of education in England and with the Government's responsibilities towards universities in Great Britain.

b.   **Welsh Office, Education Department**: schools and higher and further education (outside universities) in Wales, excluding matters connected with universities and the qualifications, probation remuneration, superannuation and misconduct of teachers.

c.   **The Scottish Office Education Department:** schools and further and higher education (outside universities) in Scotland.

d.   **Department of Education, Northern Ireland**: schools, further education and universities in Northern Ireland.

2.5   **The Universities Funding Council, UFC** (Universities Grants Committee, before April 1989) advises the Department For Education on the needs of the UK universities (excluding the Open University and University of Buckingham), and the Department of Education, Northern Ireland on the co–ordinated planning and development of the Northern Ireland universities.

2.6   **The Polytechnics and Colleges Funding Council** (National Advisory Body (NAB) prior to April 1989) advises the Secretary of State for Education on the management and funding of higher education institutions in England outside the universities. The Wales Advisory Body (WAB) advised the Secretary of State for Wales until 1992. From 1992 the Welsh Office had taken over the responsibility for colleges of higher education.

2.7   With effect from April 1993 both the Polytechnic and Colleges Funding Council and the Universities Funding Council will be replaced by separate unitary Higher Education Funding Councils for England, Scotland and Wales. Similar arrangements will also be made in Northern Ireland.

3.   STAGES OF EDUCATION

3.1   There are five stages of education: nursery, primary, secondary, further and higher education. Primary and secondary education is compulsory for all children between the ages of 5 and 16 years, and the transition is normally at age 11. However, some local education authorities in England operate a system of middle schools which cater for pupils on either side of this age, and these are deemed either primary or secondary according to the age range of the pupils. Post–compulsory secondary education usually lasts for two years. No fees are payable at any primary or secondary school wholly maintained by the local education authorities but it is open to parents, if they choose, to pay for their children to attend other schools. In Northern Ireland, children who attain the age of 4 on or before 1 July are required to commence primary school the following September.

3.2   The non–compulsory fourth stage, further education, covers non–advanced education which can be taken at both further (including tertiary), higher education colleges and increasingly in secondary schools. It can include courses usually taken in secondary education. The fifth stage, higher education, covers advanced level study including initial teacher training, which, at least for those students on full–time courses, takes place mostly in Higher Education Institutions including universities, University Departments of Education and the former polytechnics.

4.   DATES OF PUPIL/STUDENT COUNTS

4.1   Pupils and students are counted at the following dates, mainly at the end of the calendar year:

Schools   –   January – except for Scotland (session 1974/75 onwards) when the count is at September.

Further education and higher education outside universities funded by the UFC

                       –   1 November – England and Wales and FE for Northern Ireland. October – Scotland (full sessional count is also available from the Scottish Office Education Department) and 31 December for Teacher Training in Northern Ireland.

Universities   –   31 December from 1965/66 onwards – previously overall enrolments were counted.

Where pupils and students are counted at the end of the calendar year (during or at the end of the first term of the academic year), those leaving shortly after the academic year starts will be omitted from statistical returns. Similarly, those joining after the count date will not be included either.

5.   AGE MEASUREMENT

5.1   The 1982 edition introduced age measurement at 31 August, ie immediately prior to the start of the academic year, so yielding complete academic year cohorts and in particular correct post–compulsory school age data. Time series tables use the original basis of 31 December for 1965/66, 1970/71 and 1975/76, with data on both bases for 1979/80, shown in the 1982 and 1983 editions. Scotland and Northern Ireland have provided estimates for schools and school leavers; also for further education in Northern Ireland.

5.2   Table 16 still uses the December basis to avoid inflating nursery figures with 'rising fives' in primary education. Hence tables 13 and 16 are not comparable.

6.   YOUNG PERSONS' POPULATION

6.1   Population data in table 1 are derived from estimates provided by the Office of Population Censuses and Surveys. Data for 1989 and later years are based on the Government Actuary's Department mid–1989 projection, which embodies the following principal assumptions:

    a.   fertility rates, declining in the period up to 1977 and generally increasing since then, will continue to rise gradually and level off by the year 2010 at the equivalent of 2.0 births per woman.

    b.   mortality rates of children and young adults will decline slightly.

    c.   net migration will be small throughout the period of the projection.

6.2   Alternative views to 6.1.a. above may be considered when making forward estimates for the purposes of educational planning.

7.   FINANCE

7.1   The statistics in tables 5 to 7 are based on the statements of expenditure and income of the Education Departments of the four countries as included in the Civil Appropriation Accounts presented annually to Parliament; on annual returns submitted by local education authorities and educational institutions; and on the statement of grants paid through the Universities Funding Council, Polytechnics and Colleges Funding Council and to the Open University (all included in the Civil Appropriation Accounts) and of grants paid by the Department of Education, Northern Ireland, in the case of two Northern Ireland universities. Private expenditure on education is excluded.

7.2   The tables exclude:

    a.   expenditure on education by other Government Departments other than through a local education authority;

    b.   all public expenditure on libraries, art galleries and museums;

    c.   receipts and payments by the Government Departments in connection with teachers' superannuation.

7.3   To facilitate the use of the statistical material in economic and social analysis, public expenditure on education proper has, as far as possible, been separated from "related" expenditure – mainly on welfare and other amenities connected with the educational system.

7.4   The tables do not purport to show how the burden of the cost of educational expenditure is divided between the central government and local authorities. Generally, the expenditure is attributed in the tables to the authority initially responsible for making the payments. The tables do not, therefore, reflect the redistribution of the cost of the service arising from:

a.   payments by the central government to local authorities in England, Wales and Scotland of general grant and other grants;

b.   the arrangements in Northern Ireland for sharing educational expenditure between the Department of Education, Northern Ireland and local education authorities.

7.5   Throughout this publication the terms "expenditure" and "income" are used, even though in some cases the amounts, being based on a cash accounting system, are strictly on a "payments" and "receipts" basis. The latter is the case for all central government expenditure and for local education authority capital expenditure.

7.6   Amounts related to capital expenditure appear in these tables under three heads:

a.   capital expenditure financed from revenue contributions;

b.   capital expenditure financed by loans;

c.   loan charges.

All capital expenditure by central government and a relatively small part of the expenditure by local education authorities is financed from revenue contributions; most of local education authority capital expenditure is financed by loans. The gross capital formation of public authorities is obtained by combining items a. and b. The total expenditure chargeable against revenue is obtained by combining items a. and c. The latter are the financing costs of capital expenditure and they combine loan repayments and interest thereon.

7.7   In table 5, UK total public expenditure on education is expressed as a proportion of UK Gross Domestic Product (GDP) at market prices (factor cost plus taxes on expenditure and less subsidies). GDP represents the value of total economic activity on UK territory before allowances for depreciation of capital goods. An alternative comparison could be made with Gross National Product (GNP) which is equivalent to GDP plus net property income from abroad. In table 5, Value Added Tax on United Kingdom educational expenditure has been incorporated into the total United Kingdom educational expenditure. This enables the educational expenditure percentage of GNP or GDP at market prices to be calculated on a basis that incorporates taxes both in the numerator and the denominator. An additional adjustment for capital consumption, which is included in the compilation of National Accounts aggregates, is not included in the title but is footnoted.

7.8   Included under the appropriate heads in the LEA expenditure, is money received by them for expenditure on work–related further education, the Technical and Vocational Education Initiative (TVEI), and Adult and Youth Training. This money now comes from the Employment Department who from November 1990 took over the responsibility for the provision of public employment and training services from the Training Agency (formerly the Manpower Services Commission) which from that date ceased to exist.

8. AWARDS

8.1   The statistics in tables 3 and 4 have been compiled from annual returns from local education authorities, Research Councils and data held by the Education Departments.

Post–graduate Awards

8.2   Postgraduate awards in the natural and social science subjects are made by the five Research Councils in Great Britain. Awards for art subjects and other professional and vocational courses are made by the Education Departments; the Northern Ireland department also being responsible for the natural and social sciences. The Department For Education being responsible for England and Wales.

Awards to First Degree and Equivalent Courses

8.3   Students in England, Wales and Northern Ireland who are usually resident in the United Kingdom and follow full–time first degree and equivalent courses or post–graduate initial teacher training courses may be entitled to mandatory awards from their local education authority. The awards are intended to cover the full cost of fees and maintenance and are subject to deduction in respect of students' or parents' income. Students ineligible for mandatory awards because they fail residence or type of course conditions may be given a discretionary award. Similar support arrangements apply in Scotland under the Students' Allowances Scheme administered by the Scottish Office Education Department. Since 1991/92 awards for initial teacher training in Northern Ireland have been provided by the Local Education and Library Boards.

Further Education Awards

8.4   Students following further education courses may be eligible for discretionary awards (education authority bursaries in Scotland). These are usually at a lower rate than mandatory awards as they are not intended to cover the full cost of fees and maintenance.

Student Loans

8.5   In 1990/91 maintenance grants were frozen at their then current levels and loans introduced to supplement the grants. The eligibility requirement for loans are similar to those for mandatory grants. The student is required to start repayments soon after leaving the course although deferment is allowed in cases of low income.

9. TEACHERS

Initial Teacher Training

9.1   There are two main routes to achieving qualified teacher status (QTS) in England and Wales; by successful completion of an undergraduate course of initial teacher training or of a course leading to the postgraduate certificate in education (PGCE).

9.2   Both type of courses are run by polytechnics, colleges and university Departments of Education. Undergraduates complete a four year course leading to the Bachelor of Education (BEd) degree with honours, or a BA or BSc (QTS) course. These courses usually have the same basic entry requirements as other higher education courses, but they also require mathematics and English language at the equivalent of Grade C GCSE. In addition to the four–year BEd courses there are some two year BEd courses (mostly in certain secondary shortage subjects), for non–graduate mature entrants who already have some relevant experience and who have completed at least one year of HE in the appropriate subject.

9.3   Alternatively, those who hold a first degree, or the equivalent, may undertake a one–year full–time course leading to the Postgraduate Certificate in Education (PGCE). These courses also require mathematics and English language at the equivalent of Grade C GCSE. There are also a number of two–year "conversion" PGCE courses in some shortage subjects which are designed to equip students with a specialism by extending the subject study of their initial degree. There are also a small number of two–year part–time PGCE courses available in certain subjects. In addition to the conventional one year PGCE the articled teacher scheme requires trainee teachers to spend two years on a predominantly school based PGCE course during which they are awarded a special bursary instead of receiving grant or salary.

9.4   Qualified Teacher Status can also be achieved via the Licensed Teacher or Overseas Trained Teacher routes. Local Education Authorities (and some school governing bodies) can, as employers, offer a position as a Licensed or Overseas Trained Teacher to a suitably qualified applicant who will receive tailor–made, on–the–job, training. On these routes, it is possible to obtain Qualified Teacher Status after 2 years or less, depending on qualifications and previous experience.

9.5   Applicants for the Licensed Teacher route need to be at least 24 years old, and to have successfully completed the equivalent of 2 years' full–time higher education. The Overseas Trained Teacher route is open to graduate trained teachers from overseas who have had at least one year's teaching experience. In common with other routes to Qualified Teacher Status, these routes require applicants to obtain a standard in mathematics and English Language equivalent to a minimum of GCSE Grade C.

9.6   The pattern of teacher training and the regulations governing the employment of teachers in primary and secondary schools in Northern Ireland are broadly comparable to those in England and Wales. In Scotland, courses lead to the award of a Teaching Qualification (Primary Education) or a Teaching Qualification (Secondary Education). To gain a primary qualification a graduate is required to complete a one year training course. A non–graduate may undertake a four year vocational degree course in a college of education, leading to the award of a BEd and the Primary qualification. In all but some secondary practical and aesthetic subjects, intending secondary teachers will be graduates, or holders of equivalent qualifications, who will complete a one year training course. The BEd degree courses in secondary academic subjects, offered by colleges of education were discontinued in 1983.

Teachers and Lecturers in Post

9.7   The regulations governing the employment of teachers in primary and secondary schools in England, Wales and Northern Ireland require teachers to hold one of the qualifications mentioned in paragraphs 9.1 to 9.6 with the exception that in Northern Ireland the licensed teachers route is not accepted for qualified teacher status (QTS). However, in England and Wales pre–1970 graduates were accepted as teachers in primary schools, and pre–1974 graduates in secondary schools, without having to complete a course of professional training. The position is the same in Northern Ireland in relation to secondary schools, but a professional qualification is required to teach in a primary school.

9.8   Statistics of full–time school teachers and LEA colleges are derived mainly from returns completed by LEAs and in the case of grant–maintained and independent schools, the institutions themselves. Full–time lecturers in both universities and colleges are obtained by the USR directly from the institutions. Statistics of part–time teachers and lecturers in schools and in further and higher education are derived from returns completed by local education authorities.

9.9   The teachers' tables 9–11 use a count at 31 March or a date in January, with the exception of Scotland (September since the mid–seventies) and universities (31 December). The count for table 14 is at mid–January. Otherwise each category is in general counted during the first quarter of the calendar year.

9.10   Lecturers in universities cover teaching and research staff involved in academic work, while in other colleges all staff on teaching scales are included. As not all graduate staff in further education are recorded as graduates this figure is understated in tables 9 and 11.

9.11   School teachers cover all qualified staff (registered in Scotland) plus in table 14 those unqualified (limited since 1970).

10.   SCHOOLS

10.1   Schools are generally classified according to the ages for which they cater, or the type of education they provide. Schools with more than one department have been counted once for each department. Paragraph 2.2 explains the standardised terms used.

10.2   Nursery education is provided for children below compulsory school age in nursery schools or nursery or infant classes in primary schools, on either a full–time or part–time basis. Part–time pupils are counted in full in tables 12, 13, 15 and 16 but as 0.5 each in table 14 (and in table 15 for England only). Information on part–time attendance in Scotland is only collected for pupils in education authority and grant–aided nursery schools. In the independent sector part–time pupils in Scotland are counted as full–time. In England, the size of a school is determined by the number of full–time pupils on the register except for nursery schools where the size is calculated by reference to both full–time and part–time pupils aged under five, each part–time pupil being counted as 0.5.

10.3   In addition to the educational facilities provided by nursery classes, day care and some preliminary training are given in day nurseries (provided either by local authorities or by voluntary bodies), in "playgroups" set up by voluntary bodies and in self–help playgroups. Information relating to day nurseries and playgroups is not included in this publication as these establishments are registered with the local health authorities.

10.4   Primary education consists mainly of infant schools for children up to age 7, first schools for children aged 5 to 10, junior schools for children aged 7 to 11 and middle schools for children variously aged 8 to 13. Some primary schools may be a combination of these categories. In Scotland primary schools are generally classified as those catering for children aged between 5 and 12. In Northern Ireland, primary schools cater for children between the ages of four and eleven.

10.5   The structure of secondary education may vary between one local education authority and another. Most local authority areas have comprehensive schools which cater for all children irrespective of ability, and in England and Wales over 90 per cent of secondary school pupils attend such schools. Other secondary schools (modern, grammar and technical) usually have selective entry.

10.6   Special schools comprise both day and boarding schools and provide education for pupils with statements of special educational needs (see paragraph 10.9) who cannot be educated satisfactorily in an ordinary school. All children attending special schools are offered a curriculum designed to overcome their learning difficulties and to enable them to become self–reliant. Boarding special schools which constitute around 16 per cent of all such schools cater mainly for pupils with severe learning difficulties. Compulsory attendance at special schools is from the ages of 5 to 16 but in many special schools children remain beyond age 16. It should be noted that the non–maintained special school figures in respect of England, which have been included in this volume, relate to those special schools which are funded by charitable bodies and should not be confused with independent special schools.

10.7   The 1981 Education Act (in Northern Ireland the Education and Libraries (NI) Order 1986) gave the impetus to educate children with special educational needs in ordinary schools where possible. In addition to the number of pupils given in table 13, therefore, there were also pupils with statements of special educational needs in maintained primary and secondary schools (see table 17 part (ii)), independent schools, and receiving education otherwise than at school.

10.8   The large increase in the numbers of pupils at special schools after 1971 was due mainly to local education authorities in England and Wales assuming responsibility in April 1971 for all mentally handicapped children (similar responsibility passed to the NI education service in 1987). Previously, the most severely mentally handicapped children had been the responsibility of the health authorities. Under the Education (Handicapped Children) Act 1970, local education authorities took over all establishments catering for such children: these establishments became public sector schools and they are included in the statistics from 1972, either as hospital schools or as other special schools, according to their organisation.

To maintain comparability in the statistics, junior occupational centres in Scotland, attended by mentally handicapped children and administered by education authorities, were included in the figures from 1972 to 1975. Thereafter the Education (Mentally Handicapped Children) (Scotland) Act 1974 made children in day care centres and in mental or mental deficiency hospitals the responsibility of education authorities with the exception of nine schools still deemed grant–aided and they are therefore now included in all statistics relating to mentally handicapped pupils in education authority schools.

10.9   The Education Act 1981 which came fully into force on 1 April 1983 (in Northern Ireland the Education and Libraries (NI) Order 1984), abolished the ten statutory handicaps into which pupils have hitherto fallen. Instead, local education authorities are required to assess a child's particular special educational needs, providing a statement of those needs where necessary. Statistics from 1984 onwards therefore refer to those children with statements.

11.   SCHOOL LEAVING AGE

11.1   The minimum school leaving age was raised from 15 to 16 on 1 September 1972. The subsequent Education (School Leaving Duties) Act 1976 amended the dates in the year when children could leave school in England and Wales. Depending on when the child's 16th birthday falls, he/she may leave at Easter or towards the end of May.

11.2   Because of the transitional rules concerning dates which applied at the time the school leaving age was raised, the first school population figures to reflect the change were those from January 1974.

11.3   In Scotland, the main difference from the situation in England and Wales is the existence of a Christmas leaving date in addition to the summer one. This difference affects the percentages of pupils staying on beyond compulsory schooling in the respective countries. Thus the percentages shown for 15 year olds before 1974 and 16 year olds after 1974 in England and Wales are not comparable with those for Scotland.

12.   FURTHER AND HIGHER EDUCATION

12.1   On reaching the minimum school leaving age pupils have a variety of options. They may leave or continue at school, or they may continue full–time, part–time or evening study at other institutions – usually a college of further education. Those who stay–on at school or continue study at FE establishments may, after further study, seek admission to higher education courses at universities, polytechnics and colleges of further and higher education. The choice depends, amongst other things, on what examination results have been achieved.

Table Coverage

12.2   In 1990/91 the coverage of the students in tables 2-11, 22-28, 35 and 36 was as follows:

i.   47 universities (including the London Business School and Manchester Business School) offering courses of higher education of which 34 were in England, 1 in Wales, 8 in Scotland and 2 in Northern Ireland. In addition, data for the Open University are included as far as possible (12.7 refers also). The independent University of Buckingham is not included.

ii.   Further and higher education outside the universities provided in:–

a.   England and Wales: English Polytechnics and colleges funded by the Polytechnics and Colleges Funding Council, the Polytechnic of Wales, FE colleges maintained by English and Welsh local education authorities, institutions grant–aided by the Department For Education, and adult education centres (formerly known as evening institutes).

b.   Scotland: Central institutions and colleges of education funded by the Scottish Office Education Department, further education colleges and centres maintained by education authorities, and assisted voluntary bodies providing grant–aided courses of further education.

c.   Northern Ireland: Colleges of Education funded by the Northern Ireland Department of Education, colleges of further education maintained by Education and Library Boards and, up until the academic year 1983/84, when it became a university, the Ulster Polytechnic, which was controlled by an independent Board of Governors and assisted by grants from the Northern Ireland Department of Education.

There are in addition many independent specialist establishments, such as secretarial colleges and correspondence colleges which are not included in the statistics in this volume.

12.3   The major part of the finance for universities is provided by central government grants. The University Funding Council (prior to April 1989 the Universities Grants Committee) advises on the universities' needs and on the distribution of these grants, and acts as a channel of communication between the universities and the Government. Students do not have an automatic right of entry based on clearly defined minimum standards of entry qualifications, but must seek acceptance through individual applications for admission. To assist the admission process and to act as a clearing house the Universities Central Council on Admissions (UCCA) was established by the universities in 1961. Universities admit virtually all of their full–time students for first degrees and first diplomas from candidates applying through this machinery.

12.4   In April 1989 the funding of higher education in polytechnics and the larger colleges of higher education in England became the responsibility of the Polytechnics and Colleges Funding Council (PCFC). Other institutions of further and higher education are either LEA maintained or grant–aided. The Polytechnic Central Admissions System (PCAS) acts as a clearing house for admissions to full–time degree and HND courses in polytechnics and the larger colleges in England, the Polytechnic of Wales and some Welsh colleges (many of whom are funded by PCFC).

Other Points

12.5   Industrial Training Boards covering seven major sectors of industry were established under the 1982 Industrial Training Act. These are construction, clothing, engineering, hotel and catering, off–shore petroleum, plastics processing and road transport. Most Boards offer, through a system of levy and grant arrangements, incentives to employers to release their employees for courses in further education at all levels. Release may be for some type of part–time study, sandwich course, or special full–time short course (note 12.13 refers). Most other sectors of industry are covered by non–statutory training organisations (NSTOs). Their chief sources of income are membership subscriptions from employers and fees for providing training courses and consultancy. The level of NSTOs income varies as does the extent to which they can offer financial incentives to employers to release employees for further education courses.

12.6   From the early 1970's the Manpower Services Commission (later the Training Commission and the Training Agency) funded various training and retraining schemes for the unemployed or those likely to become unemployed. Since November 1990 responsibility for these schemes has been taken over by the Employment Department. The Youth Opportunities Programme (introduced in 1978) and the Youth Training Scheme (YTS) which succeeded it in 1982 (now renamed Youth Training) have provided education and training for young people aged 16–17 years. Students attending further education courses as part of their training under these schemes are included where appropriate in tables 21–24 and 26.

12.7   The Open University, financed by the Education Departments, started its courses in 1971. The University enables students to obtain degrees by studying at home by means of correspondence courses and radio and television programmes. There is a network of study centres, usually based on further and higher education colleges, to provide assistance to students, and full–time summer schools of a week's duration per course unit are held annually, often at universities.

12.8   Adult Education Centres are establishments maintained by local education authorities. Education for adults is also provided by the Responsible Bodies, which are the extra–mural departments of universities, the Worker's Educational Association and the Welsh National Council of the Young Men's Christian Associations. These establishments are often housed in premises used by day for similar or other educational purposes. They provide a wide range of courses, some of a recreational nature.

12.9 Normally, students enrolled in post–school education are counted once only, but if enrolled for two or more courses they are counted once for each separate course. However, in Scotland, with effect from October 1975, and in England and Wales from November 1976, a student enrolled in SCE/GCSE/GCE/CSE studies is counted once only irrespective of the levels or grades taken.

12.10 All students enrolled for courses leading to specified qualifications (see paragraph 13.5) are included whether or not they are following the complete course. Part–time day students attending classes which form part of a full–time course are included as part–time students.

12.11 Students from overseas are defined as those whose usual place of domicile or residence is outside the United Kingdom. Up to and including 1983/84 the definition was those students who were charged a fee at the overseas rate, plus EC domiciles who were charged at the home fee rate.

12.12 First year students (table 25) include a minority who are on a second or further course of higher education or who are continuing a course where the progression is at another HE institution.

12.13 Mode of study can be either full–time or part–time including evening classes:

a. **Full–time students.** These are those following a course of study or research to which they are expected to devote the whole of their time and which, in university, lasts an academic year or longer; and in further and higher education includes short full–time courses lasting 29 weeks or less unbroken by any industrial training or employment.

b. **Sandwich course students.** These are included with full–time students. The essential feature of a sandwich course is that the period of full–time study averages 19 or more weeks per academic year, and is broken by a period (or periods) of industrial training forming an integral part of the course.

c. **Block release courses.** These are courses for which students are released from industrial training or employment by their employer for a period (or periods) of full–time education averaging less than 19 weeks per academic year. They have been included with part–time day courses.

d. **Part–time day courses.** Students on these courses include students who have been released by their employer for part–time study.

e. **Evening courses.** Evening only students are those who attend evening courses only. Where the students also undertake full–time or part–time day study they are included under those headings. Evening students who have been released from work to undertake study are included with part–time day courses.

12.14 A revised subject clarification was introduced for university courses in 1985/86 and for other HE institutions in 1988/89 with the result that direct comparisons with data from earlier years cannot be made for tables 26 and 36.

13. QUALIFICATIONS

13.1 Examinations offered by external examination boards and moderating bodies are not normally taken before the minimum school leaving age. At that time school pupils usually take examinations in a range of subjects offered by the examining board, namely the GCSE (General Certificate of Secondary Education) which replaced the CSE (Certificate of Secondary Education) and GCE (General Certificate of Education) 'O' level in the summer examinations of 1988 – and in Scotland, the SCE (Scottish Certificate of Education) from the Scottish Examination Board). At the end of a further two years' study (one year in Scotland), further examinations are available – A/AS levels from the GCE boards and Highers from the SEB. Two or more A level passes (3 or more Higher Grades) or their equivalent are usually considered the minimum entry requirements for higher education.

13.2   a.   England, Wales and Northern Ireland: GCSE examinations were first taken in 1988, replacing the previous system of GCE O–level and CSE (Certificate of Secondary Education) examinations. The GCSE is awarded at grades A to G while the GCE O–level was awarded at grades A–E and the CSE at grades 1–5. GCSE grades A–C are deemed equivalent to O–level grades A–C (formerly "pass" grade) and CSE grade 1. (In Wales pupils also sit for the Certificate of Education).

In 1989 the AS (Advanced Supplementary) examination was introduced alongside the existing A level examination. AS level qualifications are awarded at grades A to E and are deemed to be the equivalent to half of one A level in terms of content. AS level examinations are also designed to be taken after two years of secondary study. In the tables, leavers are shown as having a pass at A/AS level if they have at least one A level or two AS passes.

       b.   In Scotland the SCE Ordinary O–grade course leads to an examination (of approximately equivalent standard to the GCE O–level) at the end of the fourth year of secondary schooling. The new Standard Grade examinations, which will eventually replace the O–Grade, will cater for a wide range of academic ability including GCSE equivalent. Examination at the Higher (H)–grade requires one further year of study and is usually taken at the end of the fifth year of secondary schooling. For the more able H–grade candidates the range of subjects covered may be almost as wide as the O–grade –it is not unusual for candidates to study five or six subjects spanning both Arts and Science.

13.3 Passes in these examinations provide the normal minimum entry requirements for the majority of courses in further and higher education. Two GCE Advanced level passes (or equivalent AS level passes) or three SCE H–grades together with appropriate passes at GCSE level or equivalent are usually regarded as the minimum qualification necessary for entry to a degree course, but the conditions of entry to particular courses vary and depend, in part, on the balance of supply and demand for places.

13.4 Data on school leavers' qualifications and destinations are collected annually using a 10% sample survey of leavers in England and Wales. The Scottish Office Education Department provide, annually, qualified school leaver data and, biennially, destination data (now based on a survey conducted jointly with the University of Edinburgh). The data for Northern Ireland now come from an annual survey (surveys were biennial until 1985/86).

13.5   Courses leading to specified qualifications, which include those leading to GCSE, GCE, CSE, SCE and degrees, are usually divided for statistical purposes into "higher" and "further" education. Those courses reaching standards above GCE A–level, SCE H–grade and BTEC National Diploma and Certificates, or their equivalents, are regarded as higher education. In earlier editions of this publication "higher" education was referred to as "advanced" and "further" education as "non–advanced".

13.6   The National Council for Vocational Qualifications (NCVQ) was set up in 1986 to reform and nationalise the vocational qualifications system in England, Wales and Northern Ireland. It is establishing a new framework of National Vocational Qualifications (NVQs) based on 5 defined levels of achievement. The first 4 levels have started operating and coverage will be virtually complete by the end of 1994. The Government's target is that 50 per cent of the employed work force should have attained NVQ level 3 or equivalent by the year 2000.

13.7   The council is also working on the development of broadly based qualifications (GNVQ) for inclusion within the NVQ framework which will prepare young people for a range of related occupations and provide progression to higher education.

13.8   The competence–based system is being extended in Scotland through a new system of Scottish Vocational Qualifications (SVQs) along the lines of NVQs. SVQs are accredited by the Scottish Vocational Education Council. NVQs and SVQs have equal recognition throughout Britain.

13.9   Universities confer their own degrees and at present, degrees in polytechnics and colleges are conferred by the CNAA which will cease to exist with effect from 31 March 1993; with effect from 1 April 1993 institutions which are granted the power to confer their own teaching (and research) degrees will be able to have the term 'University' included in their institutional title. Institutions which are not granted these powers will have to have their degrees validated either by institutions which have such powers, or by the Open University which takes over some of the validation responsibilities of CNAA. Other advanced qualifications may be conferred by various professional institutions, individual establishments, the Business and Technician Education Council (BTEC) and the Scottish Vocational Education Council (SCOTVEC). Some diplomas and certificates are conferred by the universities. Courses, mainly non–advanced, leading to Royal Society of Arts qualifications cover a wide range of subjects, including business and commerce, languages, administration, shorthand and typing and passenger and freight transport. Other non–advanced courses lead to qualifications of the BTEC and the City and Guilds of London Institute. Statistics in respect of these and other non–advanced courses are shown in table 24.

13.10   Courses which do not lead to specified qualifications are excluded from the statistics shown in table 24 but are shown elsewhere, for example in table 26.

13.11 Undergraduates are students who are either:

    a.   taking a course leading to a first degree; or

    b.   taking a course leading to a certificate or diploma (or other qualification designated as higher education); or

    c.   attending a lecture course or laboratory instruction of a first degree or first diploma standard although not leading to a qualification.

Students already possessing a first degree or first diploma who are taking a second first degree or first diploma course are nonetheless regarded as undergraduates, even though they may be allowed to complete the course in a shorter period than normal.

13.12 Postgraduates are students who are following courses which normally require a first degree for entry, and who are:

    a.   doing research work for, or taking a course leading to, a higher degree or higher diploma; or

    b.   doing other research work; or

    c.   on a course of higher degree or higher diploma standard, though not leading to a qualification.

13.13 Students who are required to possess a first degree or first diploma before being admitted to a course leading to another (eg a Bachelor of Divinity degree course which is open only to students already possessing a BA degree) are normally regarded as postgraduate during the course leading to the second first degree or first diploma.

13.14 Tables 37–39 contain information on the stock of qualifications held by people of working age. The source is the Labour Force Survey (LFS), carried out by the Employment Department, between March and May of each year, providing information on the distribution of formal qualifications among the population of working age in the United Kingdom. The information is derived from answers given by, or on behalf of, people of working age to standard questions about educational, business or technical qualifications gained. All qualifications held by an individual are initially coded but the data presented in tables 37 to 39 (taken, in the main, from the results of the 1991 LFS although data from the 1984 LFS are also included in table 39) relate only to the highest qualification held. Although the LFS covers all people of **working age**, which for men is 16-64 and for women 16-59, the data in tables 37 to 39 are for 16-59 only. This enables a more consistent comparison to be made between the data for men and women.

Printed in the United Kingdom for HMSO
Dd295627 2/93 C16 G3397 10170